The Voice

The Voice

The Voice
A Journey through the Eyes of Spirit

Based on Real People, Actual Events
and Direct Extraterrestrial Contact

Richard E. Carmen, Au.D.
Doctor of Audiology

Auricle Books
Sedona Arizona

Copyright 2024
Richard E. Carmen

All rights reserved

No part of this book may be reproduced, stored in a retrieval system or transmitted in any form or by any means electronic, mechanical, photocopying, recording or in any other form without written permission from the publisher.

ISBN 978-0-9825785-9-9

Printed in the United States of America

Cover design by Alexander Volkov
www.alexandervolkovfineart.com
(See page 180)

This book is available at special discounts when ordered in bulk.
Contact the publishing company for more information.

Auricle Books
www.auriclebooks.com
An imprint of Auricle Ink Publishers
PO Box 20607, Sedona AZ 86341

AUTHOR'S NOTES

This was a challenging story to construct because I needed to hold to the truth of events while at the same time weave in dialogue which could not always be precisely recalled. Therefore, dialogue was a relative reconstruction that characterized people I knew; other times it was used to flush out critically important points surrounding paranormal events with them. This was a delicate balance and for that reason this book is 'based on' the true story to the best of my recollection.

Names of characters were revealed when permission was granted; otherwise, pseudonyms were used. There were three composite characters (Anna, Jim and Larry). A couple composite locations and events were also utilized. For example, you'll read about Adele's remarkable presentation at the Scottish Rite Temple. That was a pivotal point to bring in many of the main characters in one location even though we all did not meet at (or attend) that specific event. Thus, all timelines of events or meeting people did not occur in their exact sequence. These elements effectually accelerated the storyline without distorting the truth of any messages; and again, is why this is 'based on' the true story.

All references to God despite the use of masculine pronouns such as "He" or "His" remain gender neutral and represent the Father-Mother Divine presence within. The term 'Off-Planet Intelligences' embraces the breadth of species in our airspace, not the Living Spirit within. I have found that 'Off-Planet Intelligence' is a less toxic term because *extraterrestrial* can provoke confusing metaphors associated with quite a range of images from scary monsters to huggable friendly entities.

And finally, all transmissions I received through the Voice were documented word-for-word—verbatim.

About the Author

Richard E. Carmen holds three academic degrees in mainstream science with a Doctor of Audiology (Au.D.) from the Kirksville College of Osteopathic Medicine. Spanning over half a century he has served the deaf, deaf-blind, hard of hearing and underprivileged. He's been an award-winning author with over 50 publications within and outside the hearing industry including feature articles, cover stories, chapters, books and peer-reviewed scientific papers. His work has appeared in top medical periodicals such as the *American Journal of Otology*; in the long-running eminent magazine *The Saturday Evening Post*; and op-ed pieces in industry publications and on CBS 60 Minutes. Richard has been a consultant to state and federal governments, participated in think-tank forums and served on eight national boards as editorial consultant and/or adviser including the acclaimed Better Hearing Institute.

Before founding his book publishing company in 1997, he authored books with Little, Brown & Company; Prentice-Hall; G.K. Hall; and Rodale Press. Through his publishing endeavors and research, he teamed up with over a hundred scholars from around the world with scientists from such renowned U.S. institutions as Harvard, Johns Hopkins, Children's Hospital, Mayo Clinic and NIH. His most successful book (in all editions) topped a million copies distributed within the hearing industry. Through Guidepoint Global, LLC, he has consulted with Fortune 500 companies on mergers and acquisitions.

By the end of 1984, he was audiologic team leader in a collaborative study with otolaryngologists pioneering a new methodology for diagnosing diabetes by means of an audiometric configuration. He and a colleague headed up a separate scientific team while he directed audiology research at the VA Hospital, Sepulveda, California. They discovered that relaxation procedures for tinnitus sufferers held promise as effective treatment.

FOREWORD

by Sergei Kochkin, MS, MBA, PhD*

"The Creator, in taking infinite pains to shroud with mystery His presence in every atom of creation, could have had but one motive: a sensitive desire that men seek Him only through free will."
-Paramahansa Yogananda

Dr. Carmen's spiritual journey is an amazing example of how each of us is an enigma, a uniquely great but at times maddening mystery, a puzzle unto ourselves begging to be solved. If we were to have ears to hear and eyes to see we might discover that there is a Divine Intelligence subtly orchestrating and whispering to us the answers to the mystery of our being in this material world, indeed the seemingly unanswerable question of why we exist at all as unique sentient beings in this vast universe within universes.

As you read Richard's startling journey, understand that we each have our own spiritual thumbprint, thus our individual path to discover. It would be a mistake to expect to unravel the mystery of your existence by following his multivariate spiritual path. Yet, there are some commonalities in his journey shared by mystics and prophets which may assist you in your journey of self-discovery.

I have known Richard for more than twenty-five years. He is a highly educated and credentialed individual schooled in the scientific method like me. There is no evidence of psychopathology or the need for self-aggrandizement in him. Yet, he experienced a number of perplexing mystical events in his life. The scientist in him wanted to explain the meaning of these paranormal events, but the scientific method is a poor tool for measuring or explaining the infinite. You cannot measure the ocean with a six-inch ruler. In fact, the scientific method is mediocre at best at even explaining the human condition. Let us be thankful that he's sharing his very personal journey. And let us hope that it will inspire others to share their own deep mysteries. In reading about the path he has taken, you might receive validation of some of your experiences as I did. This is important because as R.D. Laing stated in *The Politics of Experience*, "Reality is but a socially shared hallucination." It is food for the soul when a well-credentialed, psychologically sound individual shares events confirming

---

*__Dr. Kochkin__ is a research psychologist with a doctorate in quantitative methods and 40 years' experience in the airline, electronics and hearing healthcare industries. He has traveled to over 35 countries, given over 300 speeches and published or edited over 100 peer-reviewed publications.

happenings in your own life, because it means you are not crazy. You are not the target nor the victim of personal delusions. Richard was contacted by a benevolent advanced spiritual Being at the tender age of nine. In all likelihood this event was the beginning of his awakening. Because of the nature and quality of this contact, I can only surmise that there is a profound purpose to his life which is embedded in the Truths he now shares.

Through his personal will, he embarked on a rigorously devoted spiritual journey in an attempt to unravel the mystery of his existence. His efforts paid off. Without such effort and devotion, it's unlikely you will find the deeper meaning of your existence. If you're content with living life as a "skin-encapsulated ego" in a world where psycho-pathology has been normalized (Watts, *On the Taboo Against Knowing Who You Are*), then this book is not for you. If you feel like a stranger in a strange land and believe that it's not the best of all possible realities, then the Truths contained in this book may assist in jump-starting your inner journey.

Life contains synchronicities which are often subtle cues designed to steer you in a particular direction or inform you that you're on the right path. Be vigilant for these synchronicities and be thankful when they come into your life. There is a Spiritual Fellowship operating out of sight on this Earth plane and in the inner structure of reality. Richard's memoir is an open invitation to become part of that Fellowship. He experienced this Fellowship through advanced Light Beings without material bodies; with close associates also on the path; and through a persistent parade in his immediate environment of sophisticated unidentified aerial phenomena witnessed by many people around him. The message here is we are not alone in our difficult journey and at times we can receive help. Be watchful and mindful. The emissary of Light in your life may be a very humble unassuming soul who carries your baggage or sweeps your floor (Hesse, *The Journey to the East*).

Various spiritual journeys have demonstrated that it's possible to have a direct experience with the Infinite Intelligence and Creator of All, The Holy Spirit, The Most-High God, The I-AM-THAT-I-AM (revealed by Moses) without intermediaries and outside organized religion (though you're not asked to give up your religion). But you must want direct communication with God more than anything else and like all the sages and prophets of the past who have left you clues, you must find a way to turn off the cacophony of the world. In so doing you may possibly hear the gentle whisper of God beyond the noise.

You may even begin to discern the true nature of God which is beyond anything you can even imagine. There is a joyous cosmology behind the curtain of this material reality. Once you find that truth you will discover there is only one possible dream, and you'll want to share it with every soul regardless of perceived merit or challenges.

Richard's advanced Beings of Light transmitted some profound messages which may well assist you in your own quest. Do not be dismayed or unimpressed that the transmitted wisdom doesn't fill multiple volumes such as we see in popular channeled works. The collective messages received and transcribed by Richard contain a brief teaching, that the only thing you need to discover is The Great Cosmic Gift which is available to all. You only need to go within to find it.

Understand in your uniqueness that God will come into your life in the form most conducive to your present orientation of being in the material world. But no matter what form that may take, the goal is always the same—to help you shed this delusion of existence ("an inauthentic state of being," states Plotinus, as described in *The Enneads*) and to return you to your original Image and Similitude in perfect harmony with God.

Finally, I wish to offer one small book: *The Impersonal Life* (Joseph Benner, DeVorss edition) which made a difference in my life. I discovered it early in my own quest. I was delighted to find that its core message was captured independently in the spiritual transmissions you will read through Richard.

Matthew 7:7-8 KJV: *Ask, and it shall be given you; seek, and ye shall find; knock, and it shall be opened unto you. For every one that asketh receiveth; and he that seeketh findeth; and to him that knocketh it shall be opened.*

PROLOGUE

The search for truth wherever you look never really ends, whether personal or professional. I continue to reflect time and again throughout these decades on this wild and unpredictable expedition into the mysteries of life. When any of us look back, sometimes we see that everything rolled along exactly as we expected. You love your family with all your heart and they embrace you in ways that nourish your soul. You go to school. Along the way you socialize with great friends who you hope will remain close forever. You make progress in your education. Then early-on something happens to you, so life-altering is this event that you cannot even share it with your best friend for fear of not only being disbelieved, but full-on crazy. You hold this secret with you as life marches on and you somehow make it through the teenage years, then out of college.

But the secret keeps eating at you, reminding you that it's still brewing. It's still here. You propel through a career, work for years and build a wide range of relationships. But the backburner simmers with memories of that night alone on the sofa when an angelic Figure materialized without so much as a whisper. The warm and cozy blanket was swept off your body along with your entire perception of the world. You were held so intimately, so tenderly and loved so overpoweringly that your own spirit ignited by means of some great power right out of the center of the universe. Through the years you try to ignore it, even run from it, but you can't run from what's so deep inside you.

The time finally came for me to acknowledge the unrealized presence of something so big, so remarkable, that it ultimately answered my longest held and most existential questions: *Why are any of us even here and how do we make that higher connection?*

CHAPTER ONE

Talented front desk receptionist, secretary and office manager Doris buzzed my computer station. "Richard, call on line three."

"Hey Sid, you dog, what's happening?"

When my buddy Dion Svihovec heard me call out Sid Smith's name, he looked up from the wide berth of computers across the room. "Hey!" he shouted. "Tell him he owes me a tennis game!"

Dion and I were co-investigators. Our tight friendship dated back to 1973 when he was completing his PhD at the University of Southern California and I was finishing my master's degree at California State University. We became brothers from different mothers the first day we met at the audiology clinic. It was the era of Cheech and Chong. Often in the clinic we'd role play the comedians. One of us would inevitably knock on a wall or a door and shout, "Dave? Hey, Dave! Is that you?" as the other would throw back, "Dave's not here!" You'd have had to have been there. Just that got us laughing hysterically. While tragedy can bind friendships, laughter became our hallmark.

Dion was as authentic as his many cowboy hats. Born and farm-raised a North Dakotan with his hands on the wheel of a tractor almost before he could walk, he knew as much about wheat and barley as audiologic diseases. During those fabulous days of the early 1970s, our group would grab a few beers at the Clover Leaf and by midnight walk a few blocks to Pershing Square in central downtown Los Angeles to hang out with the street people to see if we might give them any hope. We were just college kids, young, didn't know any better, excited to live life to the fullest. One time Dion took his beautiful beige corduroy sportscoat off his back, the one with dark leather elbow patches, and gently placed it over a shivering drunk laying in a stupor on a park bench. I was impressed with his kindness and such compassion was never forgotten—a compassion I didn't always have.

The clinic was run by the highly conservative scientist Jim Stanton, PhD. What Jim lacked in spiritual interests he made up for in reputation and abilities. He was medium height with clear eyes, but sometimes slightly too intense set behind silver-rim glasses. He had silky blonde hair receding above his forehead.

As co-investigators at the audiology clinic, Dion and I published papers in our field based on our joint creative scientific work. While we were heavily focused in research, Sid had delved more deeply into the metaphysical. He was hoping to discover more about himself, Spirit and how the world within worked. I tried to maintain a balance between both Sid and Dion. One of Sid's areas of self-discovery revolved around his fate having been drafted into what he felt was the senseless Vietnam war. PTSD was ruling his life. He could see no way out. He quit his position as associate professor in audiology at a local university and was living day to day.

Our clinic was a veritable war room. Trainees ran between patients in various rooms and computers in the central station adjacent to the reception area. One of the enclosures, filled with state-of-the-art audiologic equipment contained a double-door soundproof booth for assessing auditory problems.

Sitting in the office chair, Doris palmed the desk and glided her ample body around. "Richard," she called out again, pulling back one side of her curly brown shoulder-length hair. "Your team article on the study will be in tomorrow from the publisher. They want you to proof it for publication in the spring journal."

Doris was religious and believed that having patience and being a good servant would secure her a place in Heaven. She had a great fascination for science and was as bright as she was charming. Her organizational skills might have given the impression that she ran the clinic instead of Jim.

After I hung up the phone, Jim asked, "What's going on with Sid?"

"This guy's looking for people to come over to his place to attend a special meeting tonight."

"What kind of meeting?"

I'm sure I must have raised an eyebrow just as Dion walked by. Before I had a chance to spew out an explanation, Dion interjected. "Sid called me too. Something about UFOs. This guy supposedly knows someone who's been contacted by aliens."

Jim let out a burst of hysteria and looked leeringly at us. "Yeah, right!"

"I know," Dion said with half a smile. "But at least it's a night out. Want to join?"

"Nnnnnno!" Jim mockingly responded. "Not into aliens thank you."

CHAPTER TWO

I entered Charlie Martin's cramped apartment with Dion and Sid where the living room had been converted into a makeshift mini-theater. A podium and movie screen were set up with a mix of chairs from the apartment. About fifteen people were already there. We three claimed seats in the back row. Sid removed his brown leather military flight jacket and slung it around the back of his chair. We sometimes were mistaken for brothers by our outward appearance. Sid was almost six feet. I was a few inches taller. We both were approaching forty with a somewhat muscular build and slightly disheveled long brown hair. He had a thick mustache. I had a closely cropped beard. Both of us were slightly graying at the temples.

Dion ran his fingers through his thick curly black hair and stared at Sid.

"What the hell's so funny?" Sid asked.

"You!" Dion replied.

"Me?"

I pointed at Sid's head. His bushy brown hair was pulled back into a small ponytail. Around his forehead sat WWII orange-tinted B-42 bomber aviator goggles picked up years earlier at an Army-Navy store.

Dion and I were still giggling. "You look like the Red Baron!" I said.

Sid laughed with us at his own silliness and pulled them off. Scanning the room, Sid grew a bit impatient. "I'm going to grab some water. You guys?"

Dion and I nodded appreciatively.

While Sid headed over to a table set up with refreshments, I reflected on the bond among we three amigos. Through the years we had been inspired by the works of Edgar Cayce; Nostradamus; the Ra material; Carlos Castaneda; Jane Roberts; Hermann Hesse; Zecharia Sitchin; the Zohar; books on Enoch which included J. J. Hurtak; and countless other publications on God, mysticism, the occult, prophecies, UFOs, meditation practices, fasting, diet and similar subject matter which included content from various religious sects. We would spend hours discussing our own interpretations of the mysteries of life and our own spiritual perspectives.

As young college buddies we shared a dream of becoming working practitioners and researchers. As Dion plowed into a career, Sid's life was tragically unraveling. I could not know it then, but the spirit of the Sid we once knew seemed to have died in Vietnam. Only a fragment returned of who he was. Although his fears had kept him alive in the jungle, he was wise enough to know they might destroy him at home. The ghosts of the enemy were still chasing him in what would come to feel like an endless haunt. He had to find a way to rid himself of the torment, the nightmares, the ghosts and demons shadowing him. My friendship with him was a solid shoulder on which to lean, and I appreciated his intelligence and spiritual depth. My comradery with both Sid and Dion were mutual treasures.

As Sid returned with a glass of water for us, someone turned off a corner light in Charlie Martin's apartment signaling time for the presentation. Just then a stunning brunette in her late twenties caught Sid's attention when she looked around for a place to sit. I tried to ignore my buddy's focus, but she sat down directly in front of us and placed her shawl over the back of the chair. She glanced at Sid, then at me and Dion, just long enough for me to be consumed by her beautiful eyes that ever-so-briefly locked onto me. We exchanged a warm smile and it was over. I hoped the shiver down my spine wasn't too obvious. I couldn't recall the last time a woman looked at me that way. It felt good. I missed that connection.

The lights in Charlie Martin's apartment finally dimmed along with my carnal attraction to this woman. Charlie was at a makeshift podium. He was nearly bald with thick gray-brown eyebrows and a small bush slightly protruding from each nostril. He had a round face, dark eyes and was noticeably overweight with a barrel chest down to his beltline. His speech seemed to slip out of the side of his mouth.

"I want to thank you all for being here tonight. This here is the story of Eduard 'Billy' Meier, a Swiss-German farmer and caretaker who directly communicates with extraterrestrials. I'm trying to secure rights to his story for print and audio markets and have hundreds of his photos for sale here tonight. Meier has written over three-thousand pages of material on his contacts...."

The concept was titillating. The audience was attentive and focused on every word. While Charlie continued unabated with a series of UFO slides and a pitch for investment in a documentary film on Meier's story, my mind again wandered to the gal in front of me and those eyes. They seemed more haunting than the UFO slides on screen which held everyone else's attention.

"Many photos Meier took have been documented by a Hollywood photo lab as legitimate," Charlie said. "There's been no trickery here. Meier has taken over three hundred and fifty pictures and has filmed many close-up beam-ships on his 8mm motion picture camera. His main contact is Semjase, a woman apparently from the star cluster Seven Sisters, better known as the Pleiades in the Constellation Taurus, more than 400 light years from Earth. She's telling us that our technology has exceeded our spiritual development."

Sid whispered to me and Dion, "Exceeded our spiritual development?"

"Yes," we whispered.

"And she traveled 400 light years to tell us this?" Sid queried with a smirk.

Dion couldn't help himself. "I could have told you that and I only came from Pasadena."

I motioned them not to embarrass ourselves. However, the more Charlie explained the Meier story filled with what I felt was proof of nothing, the more impatient I got. My thoughts drifted again. I had my fair share of wild flings and relationship failures. Now at thirty-nine I was beginning to think I'd never settle down and that would probably mean no children. I loved kids. Yet I knew before I could find the right woman, first I'd have to find myself. The brunette in front of me was arousing something akin to hunger. These were precisely the feelings I knew I had to get under control. I had to put it in its rightful perspective rather than letting the carnal energies of desire, lust and ultimately so much misdirection take command of my life. I was sensing that I needed to clear a path to a higher purpose by reducing these sexual distractions and temptations which thus far had brought too many challenges and misery. I had to figure out a way to gain control of my future.

Charlie's presentation was eating up short of half an hour. He was concluding. "Semjase's message is clear. We're a warring species who have lost our way. When we come to understand and realize the existence of extraterrestrial life, we will have far greater gratitude for our own lives and the lives of others."

Appreciating the underlying truths expressed by Charlie, it still struck me as just one more trite UFO story, unprovable and possibly contrived. Not a minute too soon for me, the presentation ended and on came the lights. While Charlie took questions from guests, I slipped away to the back of the room where I saw a bunch of donuts and the voluminous sets of Meier UFO photos for sale. I picked up a photo album and flipped through pictures. One after another I saw close-up shots of what I imagined could be silver ash trays or exotic hub caps thrown in the air and photographed to look like UFOs. Some looked like possible double exposures and maybe a host of complex trick photography. I shook my head in obvious incredulity, but kept turning pages. The photos were purportedly taken by Meier himself and proclaimed authentic. Hard to know. If they were real, it would be an all-time first with these kinds of images. In several photos, prominent piston-like parts were visible in startling detail. The UFO craft structure in one photo was embedded with silvery steel ridges, channels, crevices and—

"Oh, come on!" I must have mumbled to myself, disbelieving what I was viewing. I flipped the page one more time and gasped. If the entire collection was a fraud, I knew this picture was right out of my own experience. I picked up the album to inspect the image more closely. It was a UFO flying at forty-five degrees completely aglow in fiery orange-red. I'd seen the identical thing ten years earlier. I knew that if I had a camera at the time, this is exactly what I would have captured.

It was winter of 1975, around midnight when close friend and roommate Bill Schohl and I were driving north on the San Diego freeway. Around Long Beach I spotted what looked like a fireball in the sky heading at incredible speed in our direction. It was coming from the northwest horizon. It was difficult to see clearly, partly because of its speed, but mostly because of the maze of countless lights hanging throughout numerous oil reservoir tanks.

Banging the tip of my index finger into the windshield in the direction of the lighted object, I yelled, "Bill, look. Look!"

My tone panicked him. "What? What are you looking at?"

He held the car at 65 mph along the fairly deserted freeway. A cacophony filled the car from tire-road noises, wind and car rattles sailing through his '63 VW Bug. We were parallel to a huge industrial complex where dozens of high tubular smoke and flare stacks shot out tall, dancing orange flames licking the air. Hundreds of other lights atop dozens of enormous oil reservoir tanks rose at least fifty feet or higher. Because of the speed of the craft, I sensed it would all be over in a matter of seconds.

"There, Bill! Look!" I continued pressing my index finger white against the windshield. "The light!"

"Where the hell are you looking? There's a million lights!" he sharply retorted, unable to differentiate one light from another among the myriad of sparkling lights and orange flames from flare stacks shooting out from the darkness around us.

My heart was pounding out of my chest. The craft dropped from the sky toward our car at tremendous speed, faster than the eye could certainly follow if you hadn't already nailed it in the air. Bill still couldn't see it.

"Holy shit! It's coming at us! Bill! Bill! Pull over!"

While Bill pulled the car onto the shoulder, the object arched down at forty-five degrees and struck the ground without a sound or explosion on the opposite side of the freeway behind a single reservoir tank not more than a couple hundred feet from where our car sat. Traffic whizzed by apparently unaware. Frustrated and amazed by the experience, I knew those tanks were behind locked and secured gates making any investigation impossible. In less than a minute a helicopter rapidly locked onto the site. Its emergency lights were flashing. As it began continuously circling in short arcs over where the craft appeared to have crashed, it turned on a wide-beam searchlight which sharply illuminated the ground below. Apparently finding nothing, it flew off. Bill and I just looked at each other, confused.

Suddenly, a hand slapped down hard on each of my shoulders, squeezing and startling me back into Charlie Martin's apartment. I jerked around to discover Dion standing over me.

"Jumpy! Jumpy!" he said with a smirk. "What are you looking at?"

"I've got to buy this photo album!"

CHAPTER THREE

Arriving home from the UFO presentation at Charlie Martin's apartment, my head was spinning. My rumination culminated in newfound motivation to unravel one of my deepest mysteries. What had happened to me in that existential moment when I was just a young boy? This would require that I consider all things possible. This was not a new idea, but I understood that I needed to live my life with this axiom like a dangling carrot. While this consideration would be difficult to sustain because of my tendency to believe little and challenge everything, I was committed to it with the hope of garnering a greater understanding of my unexplainable, mystical childhood encounter.

I sorted through all of the Meier photos and found myself staring at that one special picture that so captivated me. I recognized the image as real as the mystical Figure from childhood who had carried me to bed. I was compelled to start putting pieces of my life's puzzle together to try to make some kind of logical sense out of what had always seemed so inaccessible—even unattainable. The fact that I had been physically raised up and off the sofa by a Figure gave me assurance that I was dealing with an entity who had obviously been physically present with me. I had to consider the impossible. That experience had been proof that *we are not alone*. My hope was that by coming to terms with this fact and opening my mind to consider that *all things are possible*, perhaps the ideas of spirit, supernatural and extraterrestrial might start to rise high enough into my consciousness that I would eventually come to terms in some rational way with what happened to me when I was a mere nine years old.

I placed the Meier photo album onto the library shelf among the many racks of books that lined the walls. Shadow, my silky gray and white alley cat who walked into my life seven years earlier, poked his head up from behind a stack of books and purred at me.

We went into the living room and plopped down on huge floor pillows in a corner of the blue and white Chinese rug. I closed my eyes and grew introspective. Change? How do I do that? I saw that my life was largely comprised of reactions rather than true 'mindfulness'—a lesson I too often neglected from Buddhist teachings about the need to always be present. I found my head was too often filled with irrelevance. I'd been engaged in repeated dysfunctional relationships, suffered from the same internal conflicts, slid into the same negative thinking, battled the same broken record—ad nauseam. I'd taken note that others seemed to be doing pretty much the same thing whether rich or poor, unemployed or powerful, famous or hiding in a closet. Worse, I realized when presented with opportunities for positive change, I didn't opt to act on them even though they could have bettered my life. A rut? My old patterns persisted out of habit and had latched onto me like the grip of a bulldog holding me down. Love relationships changed only by the different names of the women, and cities or consultancies changed only to find the same undesirable conditions of low pay and high stress. I couldn't get out of my own way to save my life, yet I felt compelled to escape. But to where? I knew my academic and career successes hid a deeper rumbling. Discontentment. Frustration. Fear. Then add a little anxiety to sandwich it all together and I found myself aching to break my pattern.

In this moment of contemplation I felt like I had dropped to the bottom of a deep, dark pit gasping for air. A breakthrough had to happen to stop the vicious cycle of frustration and despair. I knew it couldn't come from religious dogma or the possibly corrupted beliefs of others. It had to rise up as original and within me. To achieve this I just knew I'd have to view life through the innocent eyes of a child. No judgments. No rationalizations. No excuses. Just feel. Experience. Come to know Truth.

I sat with my eyes closed petting Shadow for a long time as I reflected. Dion and I had built an effective tinnitus rehabilitation program teaching relaxation and meditation techniques to veterans suffering from chronic and disabling tinnitus. Now I needed to turn those techniques on myself to rehabilitate a purposeful and deeply spiritual life. My mind was calm as I rocked back and forth on the rug soothing a somewhat lost soul.

After a while I sensed something churning deep within like the smell in the air before a big storm is about to hit. Dark clouds hover. The wind comes and stirs the air. You just don't know how big the storm will be but you know it takes the storm's arrival to get on the other side of change. Change must come from Higher Truths that give vision to a brighter future ahead. That meant breaking down every barrier, peeling away every layer of the onion. I would have to knock down every wall to find what was laying behind all the *masks* (that "inauthentic state of being") I felt I had been wearing which represented an identity that was not me, not my core, not even what I wanted anymore. My masks—audiologist, writer, researcher, practitioner—felt as forged as the imitation, multicolored, Tiffany chandelier hanging over my dining room table. This was the moment I had to go deeper. There was to be no more 'trying.' For me trying was now lying. There was only doing. But how do you achieve this?

In retrospect, little was ever good enough. Conquering my own expectations seemed to be both my stumbling block and an underlying fear of failure. Who more important in life can you fail than yourself? How do you love another person until you recognize and can accept yourself with all your faults? I knew my searches in science were not just driven by curiosity, but with the hope of proving myself worthy; and yet, all that purported worthiness seemed so fleeting, driven by my insecurities. All my work had fallen short of personal fulfillment. The harder I worked, the more books, articles and research papers I published, the better I had hoped to feel about myself. But I suddenly realized that wasn't going to happen. Year after year, something deep within me was missing. It was an unexplained craving like swimming in darkness for a raft you know is there, but you can't find it. Behind the exterior mask of who I appeared to be to others, there was an emptiness. A void. Something so buried, so hidden, not only from the world, but from me. In its own way, I felt broken.

How do you master fear of change that rises out of dissatisfaction of where you are in life? Where do you find that strength? The guts. I was no adventurer. No mountain climber. No skydiver or deep-sea explorer. I knew I was most comfortable sitting behind a stack of books and diving into analysis searching for unexpected and exciting discoveries by tabulating data and landing significant results. Yet, that yearning persisted for spiritual self-discovery that I knew must now jump off the pages from all the books I had read; go beyond all the human potential seminars I'd attended; supersede all the pop-psychology audiotapes to which I had listened. I never felt more ready. I would only have to find my way through this maze of the mind, the heart and life to muster the will and courage to move forward with meaningfully less negative everything—especially fear. I had to make a breakthrough in understanding my childhood encounter.

I transitioned into transcendental meditation by quieting the active left brain of rational thinking and calming the right brain of creative thought, seeking the center of stillness—the zone. In this process I listened to the rhythmic movement of my breathing, like the comfort of ocean waves—very slowly in and out until I moved into a deep meditative state. The process of listening to my breathing diminished self, ego and environment. Soon even my body disappeared from consciousness. While I intended to remain in this state for fifteen to twenty minutes, more than forty-five minutes passed. Taking full advantage of this deep state of relaxation and peace of mind, as I reentered more full conscious awareness, I was able to retain my state of Zen where I posed a question to myself: *what must I change to bring about the spiritual bliss I seek?*

Slowly, answers seemed to intuitively flow as if I had opened a window into this house called the soul. It felt like when the student is ready the master appears. It was my willingness, my sincere desire, a readiness. An internal Light seemed to turn on; that is, the intuitive nature of the Self in its Divine connection. In this peak experience I realized my search for truth in science had to take a shift to a search for Truth within—Truth through Spirit. I could feel an internal force perhaps best described as inspiration now pushing me in this direction. I had read so much about this process. I had studied it well. I had given much intellectual attention to it. What I had failed to do was apply it. I approached spiritual interests more as an analyst—a scientist. I had prevented myself from going deeper out of fear of not being in control.

Now I could see my failure. I listened deeply. The very lifeforce within me was screaming for recognition. The time was now to transform what had been intellectual into what would have to become experiential. I felt an indescribable inward push. It felt right. I could hear my conscience speaking. The source that knows so well what is good for you. The one to which the mind often resists. I would begin to live my life in complete servitude to the universe and do so with as much nonattachment to the world as possible. This, of course, was the path of Buddha. I no longer would need to read about it. The time had come to live it.

Suddenly, it was as if someone has pried a boulder off my shoulders. I felt a sense of freedom I had not felt in far too long. Even my breathing seemed to flow more easily. With this new understanding another realization was born. I'd been changing the wrong things—everything external to me. I had been working to change the world around me, not me. Embarking on this new adventure felt like the journey I had always been seeking. There was no question that it was fully within my grasp. I knew I would have to pack nothing in my spiritual suitcase. I would only need openness and honesty. I'd no longer have to move anywhere. After all, it was my state of mind that would have to move.

In preparation for this quest, I also knew with a knowing beyond words, a knowing from that deep, deep place within that you discover when life is about to transform itself—when that storm of change is upon you—that you must find ways to acknowledge appreciation for life itself and in so doing, create a new pattern for living. The force pushing from the inside persisted and a new direction was evolving like panoramic windows that open a view and welcome the fresh air of spring. Chills overcame me. I knew I would have to focus on letting everything in the exterior world go and bring my attention to the greater meaning of my life—Spirit within.

What are you willing to give up for this? I recall asking myself, not sure how much of this question was coming from a higher place within. I continued in meditative thought. I knew that a true renunciant was willing to give up everything. I pondered this thought for a few minutes and realized I too was willing to give up everything to find a deeper meaning to my life through Higher Inner Truths. While I knew that might not seem very practical or even attainable, it was all about intention. This realization crystalized the importance of my new quest and how much I desired to change and improve everything I could. My level of commitment was one-hundred percent.

At this crossroads I also recognized my failure at deeper spiritual development, and the frustration and void within that must be surmounted and filled. I would have to find a way to take the meditative state of the indwelling breath of life and live it fully in the world around me. Preparation of the body, mind and spirit would be required. Therefore, I presumed everything else might just fall in line. That meant becoming lactovegetarian, expressing gratitude before each meal and living a celibate life like a monk in the city. And I would have to learn to detach from all I could. The process of nonattachment would require letting go of many enjoyments and pleasures in order to succeed. That would entail no more television, newspapers, alcohol, sugar or stimulants from caffeine to over-the-counter drugs. While I prepared my body through nutritional foods, I would also have to prepare my mind. I would commit to a minimum of twenty minutes of dedicated daily meditation where I could transcend all the negative emotions of fear, anger and anxiety, and stop negative thinking with all the "can't do" and "won't do." I would need to grow my ability to love and trust again, having just set myself free from an unabated sexual attraction to a Hollywood-gorgeous but lying and cheating alcoholic woman.

In the meantime, underlying all these changes was perhaps my longest held curiosity. *Why are any of us even here?* Maybe I'd find out. This new mission not only felt right, it felt like my very life depended on it. That was my level of commitment.

At this late hour of the night my eyes could barely stay open. I had to get some sleep. I walked out into the hall, down the long Chinese rug runner and into the bathroom. I brushed my teeth, threw off my clothes down to my underwear and a white wash-worn t-shirt, got in bed and flicked off the light. I fluffed my pillows on the king size bed and rolled to the right. Just before I removed my glasses my gaze shot across the hall through the second bedroom and out the large window. An unusually colorful, huge, single star shifted back and forth—shimmering. I was so tired I was sure my nearsightedness was playing tricks on me. In all my years in that house I had been unaware of a star that big being so visible in that position in the sky. I placed my glasses on the nightstand and closed my eyes with the intention to look again in a few minutes, but in a few minutes I was asleep.

CHAPTER FOUR

In the morning I was pacing the living room floor. Above the mantle hung a large mirror where I caught the passing reflection of a very frustrated man. My past yet-to-be-explained interaction with the Figure in childhood was inching closer. My inability to clarify that encounter persisted and seemed to have been standing in my way of a deeper grasp of spiritual understanding and emerging new goals for change.

The longer I thought about the unexplainable, the more I could feel a life-force starting to swirl inside of me. My mere memory of being held in the remarkably gentle embrace of the Figure's arms ignited an almost adrenaline-like pulse through me. Something yet unknown within seemed to be directing me. I knew my old life must make way for a new horizon. This new wave moving through felt like exciting unexplored terrain. Old patterns would have to change. If I could just maintain an inner focus and direction, I knew it would bring the change I needed. I would have to trust inner guidance. That very thought seemed to stir Spirit. Chills came over me. I would have to let the winds of change take the sails and trust in those uncharted waters while I held true to all my new commitments.

How many times had I read in spiritual literature that few people live in the present moment? It was a core sutra in Buddhism. I'd seen the absence of living in the present in myself and others around me. Memories of the past or dreams of the future were distractions of the mind. It was a place where people get stuck. If I was to give a foundation to this new path, I would have to keep my mind quiet, slow my thoughts, stay in the present, eventually creating stillness from wherein Truth rises. I had read countless books to understand that when you can fully live in the moment, you stand at the doorway to the eternal and therein come the changes. Mysteries and the unknown are merely Truths not yet unlocked, revealed or discovered.

I settled down into large pillows on the floor with my thoughts on East Indian writer and philosopher Jiddu Krishnamurti. He recognized the difference between ego and the true self. In being true to himself, he touted the importance of letting go of ego gratification and identity, because holding onto it is contrary to the very path to Awakening. Who better to know about letting go of ego than Krishnamurti? He was groomed to become a world teacher, maybe even a messiah, but disavowed it all for his inner search. He came to the realization that the mind could only be free when empty of political, religious and personal attachments. These same ideas stirred in me for many years, questioning my own ego and who I thought I was. To cross this barrier from ego to egoless requires deconstructing oneself in order to rebuild Truth from the inside out as if seeing through the eyes of a child long before the facades were created which hide the true Self from oneself.

I began pondering this monumental shift. *Who was I behind all the facades?* I was given a name at birth and assumed that identity, but that was surely not who I was and it wasn't my choice. I developed a career by great influences outside myself and survived, but that was as much by circumstance as choice, and was not my true identity. I had a house full of possessions, but those as reflections of me were also not my identity. All these *things* are fleeting, temporary. Merely masks. Then I asked, *without all these distractions, who is it that hides behind these formidable walls that took a lifetime to build? What is permanent? Where is the child hiding inside?*

My existence in the outer world, the world at large, was nothing more than a stage to play out my role, just as Shakespeare had scribed. I saw that believing one's own masks had to be the illusions which hide Truth from oneself. The more you build a life, the greater the risk of believing the façade. Therein is the paradox. I knew that peeking over the walls of delusion can be scary for fear of finding an inner child who might feel like a particle of dust stuck on a raft floating in an ocean of uncertainty. However, one thing was absolutely clear. You cannot rebuild your Self from the outside in.

In continuing to peer over the wall, I saw that I had become so enthralled with myself for so long in the outer world that I never saw the Higher Truths of what lay much deeper. *What's inside?* The distractions of entertainment, career, food and sex on top of the psychodrama of intimate relationships had left little time to explore that inner world. So, I knew I had to make the leap from the outer to the inner world to discover potential hidden Truths, if in fact they were to be found. This meant detaching myself from exterior attractions, judgments, indoctrinations and to let go of the ego—the shell, the shield, the veneer, the disguise that hides Inner Higher Truths from oneself. I was certain that when the superficial fell away, what would remain standing was Truth. If this could be done, I sensed in this moment of crystalized clarity, it surely must be a pathway to the Divine.

Without pretense I was now prepared to come naked before God.

CHAPTER FIVE

After a long day at the clinic, I pulled my four-door sedan into my driveway. Three of the children from the neighborhood were waiting for me. I had previously shared the bounty of Meier UFO photos with most of the kids within days after I bought them, but these were only part of a larger trove of pictures and books on metaphysics and the paranormal which through the years I had been collecting in my library.

Nine-year-old Johnny Anderson couldn't wait to get my attention as he crossed the street, his blond hair windblown across his baby blue eyes. "Richard! Richard!" I heard as he approached, his two large front teeth prominent against his smile. "Did you bring home any more pictures of spaceships?"

"Yeah! Did ya, did ya?" appealed Johnny's comrade Logan Turner running side by side with his buddy and a hopeful smile. He was thin with black hair, an olive complexion and quite tall for only being nine.

"Nope. Sorry boys."

Johnny was relentless. He had such a wonderful charismatic way about him that inevitably put a smile on my face. "Then would you show them to us again so Kevin can see them?"

"Please, Richard!" Kevin Thomas begged, following up from the rear to plead their case.

The children were charged up, jumping over one another like deprived dogs seeing the first sight of a bone. When I unlocked the front door to my house, before I could even remove the key, the kids scooted through faster than Shadow.

"Go ahead, Johnny," I said, trying to get my key out of the lock. "You show Kevin. You know where the album is."

Before these very words were out of my mouth, the album was in Johnny's hands and the kids were down on the thick Chinese rug that spread across the hardwood floor in front of an expansive fireplace. I changed my clothes in the bedroom but could hear the kids oohing at the photos. Shadow, monitoring the activities, sat purring on the collapsed music board of the walnut baby grand piano on the far side of the rug.

Tucking in my shirt I returned to the living room. Their excitement was genuine. Kevin pushed his curly locks from his dark eyes. "Are all these real UFOs, Richard?"

"I don't know, Kevin. I didn't take those pictures. I can't say for sure."

I took two pinches of dry food and dropped them over the top of the small, mechanically aerated goldfish tank. The two little fish squiggled their way to the surface and began devouring the food.

"Have you ever seen a UFO?" Logan asked.

I knew no other way than to tell it the way it is. "Yes Logan, I did see a UFO once."

Johnny was flabbergasted. "You mean you saw one yourself? Really?"

"Not like all those in the pictures you're looking at, but yes."

Johnny slid his hand down over his face with dramatic Hollywood flair. The three boys looked at each other in disbelief. "Wow!" the kids exclaimed.

Logan pressed on. "You're so lucky, Richard. Do you think many people have seen them?"

"Oh, I don't think I'm so lucky, Logan. Millions of people around the world have reported seeing them."

"What are they?" Kevin asked.

"Well, that's a good question, Kevin. I don't know. However, I think what's important to realize is that in this huge universe in which we live, there must not only be highly intelligent life elsewhere, I hope they're a lot smarter than all of us down here."

The kids giggled. Logan's eyes lit up. "You mean we're stupid?"

I couldn't help laughing at the question. I was even inclined to agree with Logan's literal interpretation, but I also had a responsibility to the kids. "No!" I replied. "I mean there must be many levels of intelligence in our universe and judging the condition of our world, the way we treat each other as well as our abuse of the planet, I'm not sure we rank very high on a universal scale of caring for each other."

Just then there was banging on the screen door. Johnny's adorable six-year-old sister Maddie stood in front of the screen door in a billowy pink dress looking prim and proper. She had a wind-up doll's voice. "Mom says dinner now or never you guys!"

The kids all sprang to their feet and in unison hollered, "Food!"

"Get Maddie!" they screamed.

The kids shot open the screen door and chased Maddie who was well ahead of them on a dead run down the walkway to the driveway and a sharp right toward the street. "I'm tellin' mommy you're chasin' me!" she shouted back over her shoulder.

Before the children reached the end of the short driveway, although the street was seldom trafficked, I would remind them, "Watch out for Mrs. Kretchmeyer!"

Maddie, without looking back, her voice trailing off, confirmed, "She's feeding her tortoise!"

She darted across the street with the three boys in pursuit. Their father, Gene, greeted them with hugs and acknowledged his gratitude with a wave to me. Interacting with the children meant a lot. I loved the kids and they always responded with respect and equal friendship. I often dreamed of having my own children someday. In fact, it was no surprise to my friends that my favorite musical album by my all-time favorite musical group was the Children's Children's Children by The Moody Blues.

I moseyed over to the record player with that album ready to blare through my four speakers in the living room. A particular track about finding 'the one' had so often been my mantra, but now on my newfound quest, finding a life partner would have to wait. When I would sing this song, I often imagined my arms outstretched to the clouds with my heart in my hands acknowledging painful moments of loneliness. I placed the needle on the last track of side two and The Moody Blues began their heavenly harmonies. I joined in singing as I had done countless times before. *Watching and waiting for a friend to play with, why have I been alone so long?*

When I turned around, my attention focused directly through the kitchen archway to the west-facing window above the sink. It was nearing sunset and in the blue sky I could see a twinkling, the same thing I'd seen the other night at bedtime, but this time it was moving. I watched it. Curious about what this was, I walked over to the kitchen window for a better view. It looked like the brightest star, but there was still plenty of daylight. It rested low in the sky, far below the cloud line and seemed only a short distance away. I had to get a better look.

I ran through the utility room and flew out the back door just as an unidentifiable and frightening sound exploded over my head. I dropped almost to my knees while covering my ears, not sure if a bomb had just gone off. Two seconds later another roar ripped across the sky above me.

Two Black Hawk helicopters had jettisoned low over the houses like rockets at incredible speed. I caught sight of the second one. It was fully black with heavily tinted glass and no identifiable aircraft markings. They headed west in the direction of the hovering object. I raced to the grassy backyard with the noise of the choppers fading quickly. The object of light was immediately gone and in seconds so were the helicopters.

CHAPTER SIX

I'd been working at home to meet my promised publishing deadlines with Dion. By the end of the day after more than twelve hours of writing and tabulating, my head was swimming in data. Not a grain of the desktop was visible from the dog-eared volumes of disorganized books and papers scattered across my desk. A multitude of notes spread outward from my work area highlighted tasks yet to do, but I couldn't stave off an inner drive pulling me in a different direction.

I rolled the high-back leather chair away from the knotty pine desk, stood up and paced the floor. Thoughts crossed my mind, one after another—issues I needed to consider if my spiritual quest was to move forward. I reflected on the moment with the Figure in childhood when my fear destroyed the loving moment. Intellectually, I got that so much of what isn't understood in human nature is feared because it challenges one's preconceived notions about what is or how it should be. I recalled J. Krishnamurti's thoughts on this idea when our group participated in Ojai for a *satsang*—a gathering for the truth—during what he called "May Talks" back in the 1970s. He touted that what is feared becomes a self-destructive energy.

I vividly recalled my moments with the Figure in childhood and the initial deepest heartfelt connection I'd ever known in my short nine years. But it all turned to fear. My own family was loving beyond words, but that experience was a moment of love beyond explanation—a true albeit momentary paradigm shift to a higher state of the heart. Trying to find the words to explain this loving state would have been as impossible as trying to describe the colors of a rainbow to someone who's never had sight. It was as if Heaven had opened its doors. Perhaps only those who have experienced this might know its breadth.

I reflected again on my fear with the Figure. Although fear seems like it would have been a natural human reaction to the unknown, I knew as a seeker on this newfound path that I had to peel it away if I was to discover any potential deeper meaning in that experience, let alone other mysteries.

I anxiously paced back and forth in the living room. It seemed my world had become one of academic achievements and polished plaques and over time it had become an existence devoid of all the deeper connections to a higher purpose for being alive. I realized I had built a safe world around me of facades, one in which I was master and behind which I had been successfully hiding. My world was science. If I was to honestly understand my childhood experience with the Figure, I knew there could be no hiding behind these masks. I would have to rip all of them away. To face this with all the courage I could muster, it would also mean no fear in the search. I knew a seeker cannot run from the very object of the search. Therein, I intuitively understood a deeper Truth. *You cannot reap the benefits of a spiritual path you fear.*

I stopped pacing, drew in a deep breath, blew it out and reveled a moment in this Truth. It resonated. I sensed if I could really move along this journey while progressively diminishing my fears, clarity might follow. I was coming to realize how vegetarianism and eliminating all media influences and stimulations inside and outside my body were now working well for me. I was locking down a focus greater than ever before.

Over a period of time, dogged determination and dedication, my body and mind finally seemed like they were working in harmony rather than against each other. I didn't have nasty cravings. I no longer missed morning caffeine; over-the-counter remedies; sugars; radio; television or reading newspapers. My weekly 24-hour fast was now something I looked forward to rather than dreading it. I loved my daily transcendental meditations of quieting the mind for a goal of twenty minutes which often exceeded an hour. I could feel a growing inner mindfulness and peace. As a result, tranquility was slowly replacing anxiety.

Shadow was laying on top of a precarious stack of books on the desk, his eyes closed. Upon thinking of him, he awoke, looked at me and meowed. He often surprised me by how tuned in he seemed; quite the sixth sense. Sometimes it only took me thinking of him after which he'd often open his eyes and purr.

I looked into his unblinking mysterious green eyes that resembled marbles I used to collect as a kid. "So, what do you think, pal?" I asked, mimicking his meow, imagining he held some great wisdom. He purred louder. He liked it when I engaged him in conversation. He confirmed our perfect harmony with another meow. "I agree, buddy. We're going to get answers."

He rose his back hoping for a rub on the rump. While I stood petting him, my peripheral vision caught a glimmering light visible through the library window. Stars didn't look like that. I could feel the powerful muscles in the cat's hind quarters as Shadow stretched his back for more, but my eyes were locked on the night sky. The curious light moved slowly, passing one fixed star after another. Then it stopped. At that moment, Shadow's sharp claws playfully grabbed my hand, producing just enough distraction to pull my gaze from the window and away from the riddle in the sky. When I looked back, I lost my reference point and was unable to differentiate stars from the object of interest.

An unexpected loud ring of the telephone startled me and Shadow.

"Richard?" came the questioning voice.

"Sid, my man!"

"Hey, bro. The Rams—"

The telephone went dead. I tried tapping the receiver buttons, but I couldn't get a dial tone so I hung up. A minute later the phone rang again.

"Sid?"

"Yeah, brother. You hang up on me?"

"No! Maybe it's your line."

"I was saying you owe me a beer, bro. The Rams won!"

"All right! You got it!"

"How about the Good Earth Restaurant," Sid suggested. "Half an hour?"

"See you there."

Having arrived a few minutes before Sid, I took a seat in one of a line of booths along a side wall. A waitress leaned over close to me and set down a glass of water. Her long, beautiful brown locks seemed to accidentally swing down from her pretty features and brushed across me. It tickled my imagination. I closed my eyes savoring briefly in her pheromones, taunting myself, remembering what that kind of moment was like, wishing it could have been different between me and Annie, a dedicated career as a nurse at the same hospital where I worked. She was content in any environment, as good in the kitchen as camping in the wilderness. But she wasn't predictable. Thinking of Annie always brought back conflicting emotions. Perfect sex, but a crazy woman. Her verbal abuse, but then her flood of tender words that made it all go away. Her unblemished silky smooth sensual intrigue hiding a tortured soul that I was sure I could fix. Eyes that only an angel could possess but the tongue of a devil that could not be reined in. *Was that love?*

I had pondered that question over and over countless times. I thought it could be love, even in light of her denials of addictive drinking. Along with hidden bottles I discovered and threw away time and again went any hope for a future with her. It was a relationship always on the edge—enough so good but not quite good enough. That was the hook. That was the allure and my own interminable addiction.

The entire flood of memories was coming back. It was touching a nerve deep inside. Raw beauty. Special moments. The mystery. The yearning. The passion a man has for a woman. The perfect touch. A connection devoid of language. Oh, I missed that feeling now buried in some dark cavern inside me— where it could no longer hurt me. What had been the real value in it all? Love and hope had simply been swallowed up in unrealized dreams.

"Professor!" came the commanding voice of my pal, breaking off old memories perhaps best left in the past.

"Hey, brother!"

We threw ourselves into a quick embrace and our unique handshake, then sat opposite each other in the booth.

"Good to see you, my friend," I said with a smile. "Why the frown?"

The waitress came over, slid a glass of water to Sid and hustled away.

"I have one question," Sid said, pushing the menu aside, leaning forward, his voice soft, guarded and a bit shaky. "Have things been normal for you since Charlie's presentation?"

"Normal?" I thought for a second, looking at his ample brown mustache that took up the width of his smooth, narrow face and Pierce Brosnan good looks. "Like how normal do you mean?"

"Like normal normal," he said. I gripped the water glass thinking about the star I'd seen more than once. Sid was impatient. "Hey—you want a month to think about this?"

"Look, you know my life at best is never normal, let alone normal normal. Since the meeting at Charlie's, I've seen some weird things in the sky. Lights. Like stars, but I don't think they're stars."

"UFOs?" Sid queried.

"Maybe. I'm not sure yet."

"Jim thinks it's all nonsense, but you know what I think. So your life hasn't exactly been the most, shall we say, down to earth either since that little gathering at Charlie's place?"

"What are you getting at?"

Sid scanned the restaurant over my right shoulder, then left, back and forth again—searching. With a sweep of his head he turned around and quickly back with his eyes focused right on me. "I'm being followed," he said adamantly, then promptly took a gulp of water.

"You're being what?"

His eyes rose to meet mine. "Shh! Followed."

I couldn't help laughing. "Who'd want to follow you?" I asked in a hushed tone and a big smile across my face.

"I don't know who," he said with a whisper.

"You're paranoid again," I replied softly, not quite sure why I was whispering.

I turned my head to scan the area just in case. Sid's arm with an open hand fell flat across the table harder than he intended. The salt and pepper shakers jumped. In response, a tan, dark-haired and rather somber man seated alone a few booths away slowly raised his head above the row of high seatbacks, exposing half of his broad, tough face. He seemed to stare through the back of Sid's head directly at me. I ignored him; didn't think much about it and said nothing.

"I'm not paranoid!" Sid demanded in a whisper and a pause. "But even if I was, it doesn't mean I'm not being followed."

I chuckled at the oxymoronic implications of the whole thing. "When were you followed?"

"Yesterday."

"But you don't know by who?"

Sid shook his head. "What? I'm going to knock on the man's car window and ask for his ID?"

"Actually, not a bad idea!" I ran my hand down my coarse beard. "How can you be sure?"

"I went left. He went left. I went right. He went right."

"Okay—"

"I did a U-turn. He did. I sped up. He did, always staying about a half block behind me."

"Maybe he liked the sound of Subaru mufflers. Or maybe he's just driving in the same direction as you!"

"I sped up again. Then he did. Then I just pulled over and parked and he drove by without even turning his head to look at me and hid his profile by scratching the side of his fat head so I couldn't see him!"

"That's bizarre."

"I'm glad you agree!"

"I mean bizarre that you interpret this as being followed!"

Sid's voice grew slightly unguarded. "Hey, brother! On my best day I don't bury my head in books and research. I still live in the trenches. That doesn't go away. I get a gut feeling on this shit. This guy tailed my ass! And besides, this is nowhere as weird as you seeing strange lights in the sky!"

The man a few booths away again raised his head, his brow cracked above the level of the booth. He continued his stare at us.

"Just because we attended a UFO meeting? Who cares?"

Unblinking and gazing at my buddy, Sid took in a deep breath, released it slowly and tried to calm himself down. "The car had white plates. Government white plates!"

I shook my head—bewildered and dumbfounded at the possibility this vehicle could be related to the UFO meeting. We finished a quick snack at the restaurant and left. I made my way alone through the parking lot thinking on Sid's concerns. My eyes scanned and scrutinized the poorly lit lot. I was tired and my sciatica was acting up. Just before I got to my car, I stretched my arms up and looked at the perfectly clear sky. Immediately, a single bright moving white light caught my eye. It appeared to be a large, extremely bright star-like object slowly traversing the sky and resembled what I'd seen from my home on previous nights.

As I watched, I began rationalizing that it might be a satellite or a plane. However, the object began darting around unpredictably, doing zigzag maneuvers, then it stopped motionless. The light quickly faded and was lost among a myriad of stars. I was thunderstruck. Satellites don't do that.

CHAPTER SEVEN

Around 1955—it went something like . . .

I was maybe ten years old sitting on the floor in our den. My eyes were glued to the black and white television screen where on some program the Maharishi Mahesh Yogi was being interviewed. He was describing the process of transcendental meditation—focusing on a mantra. However, he went on to describe how the mind is so powerful that it can control the body, like the major organs.

"So, you're saying the mind can control your body just by willing it?" asked the interviewer.

"Yes," said the Maharishi with a glowing smile. "Anyone can do such a thing with the mind. You see, you can control the heart and the blood flow anywhere in the body like you control your thoughts in the mind." I watched intently, never having heard such a thing. I sat upright on the floor entranced by the sing-song East Indian accent of the Maharishi. "Yes, of course. It's that easy. Yes. You want to try transcendental meditation?" he asked the host.

"Well, maybe you first give us a demonstration of how to control blood flow."

The Maharishi sat on the floor wrapped in a two-piece sarong and settled into his lotus position. His bare arms rested across his knees and his hands moved into a meditative pose. Within a matter of minutes, he restricted blood flow in one arm and increased it in the other. He explained what he was doing, but in the absence of color, it was not visible on the TV screen.

"That's amazing, sir."

"Not amazing. It's the mind that is amazing," he said giggling. "Easy thing to do."

Through pure innocence and the naivete of youth, I never doubted that I could replicate it. I turned off the TV and assumed the same posture as the Maharishi. My skinny legs easily slid into the full lotus meditation pose of padmasana. I placed my arms across my knees, set down the proper hand position and upright posture and closed my eyes. I began to concentrate unlike I'd ever done before. In my mind I was commanding blood to decrease in my left arm as I commanded it to increase in my right arm. I held a visual image of decreased blood flow in the left arm and increased flow in the right arm.

In a matter of a few minutes, I opened my eyes. It seemed I had achieved this curious thing that the Maharishi had demonstrated. Just as I made this discovery, looking back and forth from my right to my left arm, my younger sister Joy walked in.

"Richard! What are you doing?"

"Look at my arms. Do you notice something different about them?"

Bending down over me Joy inspected my arms. She could see the difference in coloration. "Ohhh! What did you do?"

I had never heard of this technique, so the best I could do to describe it was to perfectly mimic the musical flow of the Maharishi's words. "I t'ink it's called meditation! I t'ink I changed da blood flow in da arms wit da mind!"

Joy stared at my arms with a frown, and suddenly shouted, "Mom!"

CHAPTER EIGHT

I sat in my library engrossed in a book on Hinduism. *The Adagietto, 4th Movement of Mahler's 5th Symphony* softly played in the background. I'd spent the better part of a week buried in more data collection from my human studies research project with Dion and the large co-investigative team, so exhaustion was washing over me. My library looked like the aftermath of a cyclone. Tattered notes were spread across my desk among multiple dog-eared books. I had texts from the UCLA library on hearing loss and disease, all buried atop other research work piled helter-skelter across the floor. Despite the disarray, I knew where every scrap of paper, every memo and every item lay.

I turned off the desk lamp and massaged my head. I was done for the night. I walked into the living room with Shadow on my heels, gave the goldfish a couple pinches of food for their after-midnight treat and paced the floor back and forth in front of flickering coals in the fireplace. Mahler's piece finally ended. Except for the crackling fire and my own soft footsteps, the room was quiet.

I stopped in front of the mirror above the hearth. I removed my glasses and looked deeply into my blue-green eyes. There was a very frustrated man in that reflection. I hadn't yet come to terms with solid spiritual understanding about my childhood encounter which still seemed to be holding me hostage. However, throughout all this mental anguish I felt a deep connection to spirit rising within me. Something was moving. Something was changing, though I didn't yet have words for it. Lost in the reflective moment, my face disappeared from the mirror as my nine-year-old self came into view asleep on the living room sofa at our home in Syracuse, New York. It was well past midnight. The room was dark. I reconstructed the moments to the best of my recollection while also imagining the unknowns so I could fill in pieces and better understand exactly what had happened to me in 1954.

Howling wind was thrashing rain against three huge picture windows in the living room, tugging at my dream, pulling me from the lull of sleep. I was stretched out across the sofa. I'm sure my mind drifted between a dream and wakefulness. Suddenly, I sensed something was different. Snuggled beneath the safety of my favorite checkered wool blanket, a dull flickering glow must have reflected off my face. I'm sure I partially awakened, maybe leaned up on an elbow and chewed on the moment. Peering upward I might have stretched, but my eyes remain closed.

A soothing vibration seemed to be calling to me in a language of its own. It was persistent. Again, I must have been stirred from the dream. The turbulent wind outdoors grew calm. Laying in twilight sleep I sensed a presence. I imagined this must be my mother discovering me on the sofa. I expected her to stand me on my feet and walk me back to bed. I didn't want to go. I must have been having such a wonderful dream.

Laying between twilight and wakefulness, what looked like golden emanations of sunlight penetrated my eyelids. I was drawn toward this light like a moth to brightness. I was completely secure in this surrender. It was easy and natural, like being at the beach standing at the ocean with outstretched arms and not a worry or care. The light itself seemed to be creating a loving calm and penetrating gentility that filled every pore in my body. The very deepest feelings of love had in some way magnificently electrified my body. It was as if my heart had opened. I had never sensed such a thing. Every cell, every living aspect of me held this loving resonance. It was in every sense heavenly.

An arm suddenly slipped beneath my body and under my lean thighs. Then another arm glided gently below my skinny back and shoulders. One arm took hold, then the other. Without warning I felt myself effortlessly and silently whisked off the sofa and embraced in the arms of this Figure. I could feel the checkered wool blanket slide off my body. It landed in a heap on the carpet. I felt a profound loving connection to whoever this was embracing me, unlike any of the deepest feelings I'd ever known for anyone or any thing.

Fully embraced in the arms of the Figure, I was sure golden emanations lit the way across the living room to the flagstone walkway. I could still see the glow through my closed eyes. But then my rational mind started analyzing the situation. If I was being moved in the middle of the night, what was this sunlight? I was every bit certain of my father's strength, but I knew this wasn't my father. He'd been unable to lift me like this for some time. This was surely not my mother either. She hadn't been able to carry me to bed in years. Besides, if this was mom, where was her familiar scent of strong black tea on her breath or the whispered soothing *shhh shhh shhh* as she used to carry me to bed when I was younger? I was perplexed and stuck on one thought: *who is this?*

While this question persisted, the loving, overwhelmingly tranquil moment was becoming untenable. Alarm rapidly accelerated within me and overtook my vulnerable heart. My Roy Rogers pajamas tight down to my toes could not contain my feelings of helplessness and vulnerability which like a flood overtook the love, tranquility and splendor I was experiencing. I had to open my eyes and see who this was. Try as I did and try again, I couldn't. A tortuous wave of panic thundered through me.

Despite the rapidly growing almost torturous fear overcoming me, looking back, I knew something had triggered a previously unknown and immeasurable depth of love in me which I had never felt before. However, I was experiencing love succumb to fear. I was awash in deeply conflicted emotions.

What's happening to me? ricocheted over and over in my thoughts as I was methodically carried to the end of the flagstone walkway. I was trapped. I had to escape. I tried to turn my head to see what was happening, to see who this was, but there was no escape. I couldn't move my body. Nothing worked.

Swallowed up by the terror of not knowing who was carrying me and my inability to open my eyes, in a single, planned, powerful force from deep within, I struggled to collect a strength that would free me from my captor, but I couldn't even twitch a muscle. Caught as if in a nightmare, I remember releasing a scream, blood curdling and frightful as it was desperate, but not a sound came out.

Uninterrupted, I knew the Figure was heading toward the corridor that led to the bedrooms in the back section of the house. I didn't need the brightness still penetrating my eyelids to illuminate the way. I knew exactly where I was. I was taken left, then sharply right. I was being carried past my parent's open bedroom door.

Daddy! I remember screaming, but still my vocal cords were silent.

And still each frantic attempt to open my eyes failed. My heart was racing out of control. A film of perspiration expanded across my brow. I knew we were nearing my sister's open bedroom door. Then past it. *Joy! Joy! Ohhh what's happening to me?* I was screaming from within, but in the dead of night the echoes of my voice were only in my head.

The smooth whooshing footsteps beneath me were audible. I knew I'd be approaching my older sister's room. I could see her hand-painted cardboard sign tacked up on the closed door: ALL BOYS STAY OUT! She was my last hope.

Joanie! Help me! Oh God! Please help me!

Carried across a toy-filled room to my bed, I was paralyzed in the moment, locked away somewhere deep inside myself, frightened to death. Beyond reason. Beyond logic or hope.

While my lanky body was lovingly held across the Figure's powerful arm, the light that pierced my frozen eyelids was brighter than ever. It was apparent that someone was directly over me, motionless, watching me. The distance between light and dark seemed to blend into a singular coloration of life with no purpose. No meaning. No understanding. Everything frightful spilled out from this unexplainable helpless moment. My body seemed to hover above the bed still in the Figure's arm. Life itself became suspended, even surreal. Nothing mattered, and yet, everything mattered, all at the same time.

Then, the crinkling of fresh sheets and the crackling of static from the wool blankets filled my ears while the covers were pulled back and I was ever so gently lowered into bed. I felt the blankets pulled up until they reached my chin where they were gently tucked back with the sheet folded over the wool—just the way I liked it and exactly the way mom did it.

Slowly, the bright golden light began to fade with the sound of whooshing metered footsteps becoming more and more distant as the Figure left. In a matter of seconds, it was completely dark and quiet except for my uncontrolled panting. My fear was palpable. Terror seemed to lay in the stillness.

A sudden gust of wind against the bedroom windows almost seemed to be rising from deep within me and only further chilled the moment. I quivered, feeling alone and confused. Surmounting my sense of isolation my eyes popped open. They worked. I could see. I was convinced by some miracle I had eluded death. The realization of what had transpired took hold like the release from the grip of a monster. Without a moment's hesitation, reflexively, I again screamed at the top of my lungs, every vocal cord wailing, every heartbeat turned into raw fright. Tears flooded my cheeks.

It seemed like an eternity before my mother finally reached the bedroom, throwing on the light, alarm across her face at the sight and sound of my panic. I was still panting like a mad dog. It was so out of control.

"Richard! Richard honey," she called to me calmly, although unnerved by my relentless screams. She hurried over and embraced me. Trying to calm me, she held me tightly through the blankets. "What is it, honey? What happened? What happened?"

Frozen beneath the covers with my head buried, I continued hollering. "Mom! Mama! Oh Mama!"

Peeking out, I grabbed hold of her, trying to control my sobbing; catching my breath so I could tell her.

She cradled me to her as if fending off some invisible intruder. "Darling, it's okay. Calm down now, I'm here. Did you have a bad dream, sweetheart?"

I was nearly incapable of speaking, choking on my tears. "Oh Mom, I'm so scared! I'm—I'm—I'm so scared!"

"Honey, it was just a bad dream, that's all," she said with such compassion and understanding.

I buried my head into the warmth and safety of her soft embrace. A long minute passed as she soothed me, massaging my neck, calming me. I looked up at her, concerned that I wouldn't be believed.

"Mom, it wasn't a dream. Something carried me back to bed from the sofa."

She stroked away tears from my cheeks and reassured me. "It was just a bad dream, darling."

I sat up tall in bed. "It wasn't a dream, Mom. I fell asleep on the sofa again."

My father entered the room tying his robe. "Your mother and I didn't see you on the sofa tonight, son. You've been in bed all—"

"No Dad! No, I wasn't. I wasn't! Please, please believe me. Dad!"

From the doorway, Joy held onto Joan. "What happened?" Joan timidly queried.

Our father turned quickly and lowered his sight to the girls standing in the doorway. "Now you girls go back to bed. Right now! Rich just had a nightmare."

The girls reluctantly returned to their respective bedrooms.

"Dad, it wasn't a nightmare. I'm telling you. You were watching Texaco Star Theater. Milton Berle was pretending to be a girl. I heard it in the living room. I was on the sofa. That's the last part I remember."

My parents looked at each other. They knew I was absolutely correct about the TV show, but my father dismissed it.

"If you fell asleep out there, you must have walked yourself back to bed, son. That's all."

My mother locked my curly brown hair between her fingers and gently pulled my head to hers. "Look honey, you've got to be up early for school. You must get some sleep now. Put your head down and close those sleepy eyes."

I threw the blankets over my face, mumbling to myself. "Someone carried me back to bed tonight. Someone did."

My father opened one of the bedroom windows for air. "Dreams sometimes can seem very real, Richard."

I'm sure my mother must have looked at dad with a questioning eye, not so willing to dismiss what their son was suggesting, but fully incapable of understanding how such a thing could even be considered. Impossible! The idea of anyone carrying me back to bed was simply ridiculous. She pulled the blankets away from my face, leaned over and landed a big kiss on my forehead. She then pulled the covers up to my chin and folded the sheet over the top of the wool blanket.

"Shhh shhh shhh," she whispered soothingly, rubbing the palm of her hand along the side of my face and removing a remnant tear from my cheek with a sweep of her thumb. "We love you, darling. Try and sleep now."

I listened assiduously. My parents flicked off the light and my father's flip-flopping slippers faded away, distinctly different from the Figure's footsteps only moments earlier. I released a gasp of air in quiet bewilderment. The thought was still terrifying to me. How could I make my parents understand what happened? And if they didn't believe me, who would? My perplexity faded into the haze of a deep sleep and into the cold fall night.

In the morning, I clearly recalled the prior night's events. I finished washing up and joined my sisters around the large pine table in the breakfast nook. I poked at my hot bowl of oatmeal without conversation. Lost in thought I stared at the tall birch panels facing me. It was as if time had stopped. I was still back in the arms of the Figure.

My sister stared at me with disapproval. "Mom!" Joan hollered. "Richard's picking at his food again!"

"Now, you all better hurry up or you'll be late again for school, you hear?" she demanded, preoccupied at the stove.

"Mom?" I mumbled. "I know what I'm gonna be when I grow up."

"And just what is that young man?"

"A scientist."

"A scientist?" exclaimed Joy and Joan in unison, laughing.

"Well, I am. I'm gonna prove things," I said adamantly.

Joan looked at me with some disdain. It was merely the growing pains of siblings. "How 'bout proving you got oatmeal on your face!"

Used to my older sister's razzing, I responded. "You got oatmeal on your butt, Joan!"

I left the kitchen and padded barefoot down the cool flagstone walkway. Midway through the living room something caught my eye. I turned. Stunned and even disbelieving for a second, I saw the checkered wool blanket from the night before still piled in a heap on the carpet, exactly where it had slipped from my body.

Frozen in my gaze, I ran over, dropped to my knees and picked up the blanket. I crawled beneath it, hiding my entire body. I squeezed the prickly wool ever so tightly and pulled it to my chest in confirmation that yes, indeed, the encounter had been real. The profound moment of love beyond anything I'd ever known was fresh in my memory. Tears streamed down. I had imagined nothing. Yet I was acutely aware how an ocean of fear while in the arms of the Figure had washed away all that love. *How was such a thing possible?* Feeling completely alone in my futility, I knew I would probably never be able to share this experience with anyone. *Who would believe it?*

Shadow's meow brought my face back into the mirror. I snapped out of my drift from the past and was again eye-to-eye with myself. One thing was for sure. The facts and the truth were elusive and I still didn't have enough answers. Searching my disappointing eyes in the mirror, with compassion in my voice and a sense of failure toward greater resolution, I whispered to the nine-year-old boy now gone from the mirror. "I'm sorry." I was sorry that I let fear consume me.

I began an intense analysis of this childhood encounter. My memory was vivid in recalling how I had been swept off the sofa and the feeling of the checkered wool blanket sliding off my body while I was raised into the embrace of the Figure. I recalled the Figure being solid because the embrace was so firm. The only way in or out of the house would have been through a door or window. That hadn't happened because I discovered the next morning no perimeter had been breached.

So, reconstructing the moment, the entity may have entered the house through solid walls. Envisioning myself held in the loving arms of the Figure,

I tried to understand how my emotions transitioned from such heartfelt passion to utter terror. I felt I had been completely open, vulnerable, at pure peace with self and God. It was extraordinary. Being in the arms of this Figure was like being in the arms of a long-lost loving family member finally returning from war—the emptiness filled. The void gone. Since this connection to the Being was occurring simultaneous to the embrace, I assumed there had to be some history between us. It felt that way. I just didn't know what that was. I surmised that the remarkable radiance of love I initially received was also reasonable evidence of the benevolence of this Being. Proof was that no harm had come to me. I recalled a simultaneous sacred connection when golden light pierced my sealed eyelids.

Now looking back so many decades later I could not be sure if this sacred connection originated from me, the Figure or both of us. It was an enchanting moment of love completely devoid of language. The fact that such extraordinary bright light continued throughout the presence of the embrace with the Figure brought up one other possibility. From all the years of reading and learning about the deeper mysteries of life, I had read many books that talked about Beings of Light. I sensed this consideration was the most reasonable explanation. After all the decades that passed since the encounter, I realized that the transition to fear was my own doing. It was terror initiated by what I could not understand. I misinterpreted an existential event based on raw human emotions. However, metaphorically, how could a child be expected to see beyond his inability to open his eyes?

Thoughts were whirling. I needed all things considered so I flipped the scenario around to a darker possibility. I couldn't help wondering if the entire experience might have been a misconstruction within my own mind. A deception, especially understanding that the Figure prevented me from opening my eyes to bear witness to its very physical presence. Thus, I reasoned, had my eyes been sealed closed because this was a completely alien entity of such frightening physical stature that it would strike utter terror into the heart of a child? Delving deeper into these considerations, was it possible that a creature which we might construe as physically horrifying might in fact still possess the ability to connect heart to heart with a human being? In order to achieve such a loving connection without frightening a child, might it have required keeping my eyes closed? Any which way I sliced this up, the most unanswerable question persisted—*who was this Being of Light?* Where was the truth?

I picked up the 12-string guitar, sat on the Chinese silk-wool rug and closed my eyes. My fingers carried out melodic notes I had composed which moved me into a meditative state. My fingers continued to move slowly up and down the strings along the guitar neck. My thoughts drifted as rote memory took control of the guitar. Shadow rubbed his sleek body against my knees, then scurried away, but I was lost in the enchanting sounds, soon unaware of the guitar I was playing and even the room wherein I sat. By this late hour, light from the moon passing through the large pine tree branches would be shooting through the window and onto the rug. It would have highlighted the lavender and cranberry hues and probably cast Rorschach images onto the coffee table near me.

From the blissful feelings of the moment while drifting in peaceful surrender and solitude, another feeling overcame me. I stopped playing the guitar. I never quite felt this sensation before. With a sixth sense I felt I was not alone. An energy had entered the room. I opened my eyes wide. Shadow was nestled into pillows near me. Surely, he'd have been alerted if something was going on. I dismissed it as an overactive imagination.

However, something indeed was going on. Unaware, I closed my eyes again trying to lose myself in the music, but something kept pulling at me. Calling to me. Nudging me. I could feel it. I could feel it like a distant drumbeat—a distant voice. I opened my eyes again, put the guitar down and was literally frozen motionless in the sudden stillness and diffusely lit room.

Sitting in place, only my eyes moved, panning left and right below a furrowed brow. I visually scrutinized the large brown corduroy couch, the antique oak hat rack, the old pine table and chairs in the dining area and a huge brass plant bin. Everything was in its place, undisturbed, perfect; yet, I could not shake that feeling.

Something was in the room. The wind outside picked up and chills raced through my body. The hair on my entire body seemed to want to push through my clothing. Something was happening. Unmistakably. I closed my eyes and put myself into a lotus position. Shadow's eyes opened and fixed on me. He quickly ran over and sat on my lap. The sense of something in the room was overwhelming until I realized what I was sensing was not in the room at all. It was in me—deep, deep inside maybe where Spirit lives. Where imagination runs. Where God may reside.

Quieting my mind, I breathed in relaxation and blew out all concerns on every exhalation. I continued slow rhythmic breathing and soon a tremendous force passed through my body like the upsurge of a wave racing to overflow from within.

In this moment, my ever-searching self was receiving a telepathic message. It was faint but clear and seemingly coming in on every vibratory pulse of my heart. Louder and louder.

"Palm Springs—" I heard above the purrs from Shadow. "Twentieth October. Come alone. You will create a landing base."

It was over. The high electrical charge dissipated. Immediately I was left with overwhelming emotions of excitement and fear, and an inner knowing that what I had just experienced was in fact not my imagination, nor was it my own inner voice. I began analyzing it. Someone or some *thing* had just spoken to me. It was obviously a telepathic voice I received. There was nothing about the quality of it that I would have identified as being spiritual. I wondered if it might have even been computer generated.

I grabbed a notepad on the low coffee table beside me and wrote down the message verbatim and the exact date: Sunday, October 20, 1985. The only missing element in the message was the time, but somehow I knew it would be between midnight and six in the morning. I didn't even know how I knew that.

If I accepted this invitation scheduled for three months hence, I'd have to head out Friday evening the nineteenth. This was going to take every bit of courage I could muster because of the risks and unknowns. I pulled up an Afghan my mom had made for me years earlier. I slid it over my exhausted body, up to my chin and relived this remarkable moment trying to understand the implications of this potential encounter.

CHAPTER NINE

The following evening in my library while diligently making progress on my research study, I felt a tingling. I sat straight up in the chair, leaned forward and slowly parted the sheer curtains above the desk. Four stars were stationed in the dark sky. They appeared to be pulsating lights, almost breathing. The lighted vessels began a series of erratic movements, then stopped. A rather sharp prismatic clarity in radiant spinning colors of red, orange, yellow, green and blue reflected off each vessel. I was mesmerized.

Suddenly, the sound of the doorbell startled me. I ran to the living room, flicked on the porch light and swung open the hardwood door. Kevin's father stood expressionless on the other side of the screen door.

"Larry, come on in."

He stood motionless. "Look! You stop this crap of showing my kid pictures of flying saucers, you hear me?"

"What are you talking about?"

"Haven't you showed him photos of UFOs?"

"Yes, of course, but Larry, I meant no harm by it. The kids were excited to see them. I didn't think there was any problem in the kids looking at pictures that may or may not be authentic."

"You know that shit isn't real! Why do you even put that in their heads?" he demanded with distain, scraping the bottom of one of his red-dyed Abilene rawhide boots on the walkway, like a bull readying itself for the charge.

"All things are possible, Larry."

"I think you're imagining things dude! You—"

"Larry, your belief about something has nothing to do with the truth of whether it exists. I felt the kids were capable of coming to their own conclusions."

Larry pumped his index finger at my face with a warning. "Not when you mess with my boy's mind!"

Although I only knew Larry as a neighbor to throw a wave to, I couldn't have predicted such hostility. It unnerved me. I could sense the rush of adrenaline shooting through him. His face was flushed red as his boots. But I wasn't angry as much as disappointed that Larry thought I'd ever purposely deceive the kids.

"I'm not going to argue with you, Larry. And I don't need to defend my good intentions. I've looked after Kevin and the kids in the neighborhood like they were my own kids."

"Then stop bull-shitting them with your stories!"

"They're not stories, Larry." Just then I saw two of the four lights in the sky. "Turn around Larry and look in the sky behind you." I walked outside, stood by Larry and pointed. "See that set of two stars?"

"They're stars!"

I was certain Larry had no idea where I was directing him with all the various stars in the sky. "Do you know all the constellations? Can you be certain what you're seeing are only stars?"

We gazed at the sky for several seconds. Larry said nothing. The lights did not move. Larry turned back to me. "You're whacked, man! My kid is not permitted on your property anymore!"

I was boggled watching Larry storm off into the dark night. I wondered how this could have happened. I couldn't understand how the vessels could be bouncing around catching my attention and then just stop when I showed Larry. I felt foolish. If I couldn't be certain what I was seeing in the sky, and if I couldn't even show a neighbor what I myself was witnessing, a new realization came to me. *Not all truths can be shared*. It was the only logical conclusion. Was that the intended message for me?

Still in a bit of a daze, I realized my telephone had been ringing.

"Hey, brother!" came the excited voice.

"Sid!"

"I'm going down to the Scottish Rite Temple tomorrow night to see an incredible medium."

"The Scottish Rite Temple?"

"It's a Freemasonry nondenominational spiritual center down in San Diego. Want to come along? I'll pick you up."

Coming off the heels of my upsetting conversation with Larry, I wasn't in the mood for another paranormal experience. "Absolutely not!"

"What do you mean? You've never seen this woman."

"Come on, man! You know most channelers are outright fakes!"

Our conversation was brief. I stood motionless, thinking about what had just transpired in my conversation with Larry. I saw the irony and my foolishness. My reaction to Sid's invitation to attend a session with a medium was no different than Larry's reaction only minutes earlier to me suggesting that some stars may not be stars. If I couldn't move my path forward living the very Truth that *all things are possible*, I knew my quest was over. I had to keep an open mind.

CHAPTER TEN

A bit chagrined, I stood beside Sid, blinking amidst his cigarette smoke. Anoeschka von Meck, my shy and impressionable seventeen-year-old niece from Namibia was frowning at him. He read her expression and put out his cigarette. The three of us entered the Scottish Rite Temple to scout out a good place to sit. It was buzzing with more and more people filing in around us. More than a hundred chairs were set up.

"You'll love this, I promise," Sid said to me and Anoeschka, directing a mischievous wink to Anoeschka. Her blushing beet red porcelain face framed her sparkling sapphire eyes that held the look of mystery that certainly depicted her. "Adele is something else," he said.

I included my niece on this trip to San Diego after her insistence that she could handle delving into potentially otherworldly considerations. I knew how much she loved me and with such admiration looked up to me as a mentor. That held its own level of responsibility. I extended a loving arm around her with a reassuring smile. She returned the same affection.

Anoeschka spotted available seats a couple rows back from center stage. She threw her long blonde hair back across one shoulder and in her deep South African accent, exclaimed with excitement, "I see three seats!"

Sid and I approved. The three of us headed over to claim the seats. On our way Sid teased me about the adoration my young protégé clearly had for me. Once we settled in, I turned to Sid with a mock Swiss-German accent. "Is this going to be like an evening with Herr Eduard Billy Meier?"

Before Sid could reply, a brunette sitting diagonally in front of me turned around in her seat and folded her hands one over the other with her colorfully painted fingernails hanging over the back of her metal chair. She looked directly at me. "Did you say Billy Meier—the Swiss contactee?"

Anoeschka giggled anxiously.

Once again, I found myself staring into the penetrating hazel eyes of a beautiful woman. It was an instant connection. She was striking. In unison, both Sid and I responded, "Yes!"

I was overwhelmed. Something about her just tugged at me. She was radiant. It was like the excitement of meeting an old friend. It was strange and yet remarkably comforting. My attraction to her was far beyond anything physical or even her fine taste in apparel. Her skin was silky smooth—maybe perfect. She had well-defined small features and bright teeth that enhanced a glowing smile. Her tornado of dark chocolate hair was a thicket of dangles which encompassed endlessly long curls that fell far below her shoulders. It all rang of familiarity arousing an instinct in me in the absence of rational thinking.

I had to know more about her.

I leaned forward, staring into her sculpted face. "So, you know about Meier, too?"

"I do," she replied, furrowing her brow, squinting as if trying to place me. "I mean I haven't studied it like some people, though I know he's claimed contact. Do excuse me, gentlemen, for jumping in like this," she offered with a beam, "but it's not every day you hear Billy Meier's name mentioned. I didn't mean to interrupt."

"No! That's quite all right," I replied, then introduced myself.

"Jo Stone," she responded, extending her hand straight out for me to receive.

"Nice meeting you, Jo Stone," I said with a smile, not removing my gaze from hers. It was instant connection, but I had a feeling it was more than that. Eyes still on Jo, I tapped Sid in the chest with the back of my hand. "This is my good buddy Sid Smith and my beautiful niece Anoeschka."

We three adults exchanged pleasantries and chatted briefly about Anoeschka's temporary stay in the U.S. for academic purposes. In the meantime, I tried to peg Jo's speech pattern. "Do I detect an eastern accent?"

Her alluring hazel eyes seemed to look right into me. "Boston. Actually, my family used to shuttle between Boston and our summer home in Falmouth."

"Oh, sweet," I responded.

The gentleman seated next to Jo turned around in his seat, eager to engage in this evolving conversation. "Hi! I'm Rick Hurst," he said quite affably, his hand reaching out to me. "I'm also interested in the Billy Meier story!"

"Oh, I know you!" Anoeschka blurted out with her full-on, Hollywood-infatuated, beet red face again.

Rick was a successful actor quite well-known for his role portraying Deputy Cletus Hogg on a popular television series, The Dukes of Hazzard. He was naturally entertaining as he went into character keeping all of us laughing. Although Anoeschka instantly recognized him, I had never seen the show. He was late thirties, warm, stout and every bit likable.

"I just met Rick," Jo finally clarified. She furrowed her brow at me after some brief chatting. "Have we met before?"

Her very question tantalized me. Maybe she felt the same thing? Had I ever met her I knew I'd have never forgotten that meeting. A tingling ran through my body.

"I don't believe so," I answered.

"Maybe a former life?" Rick suggested with a broad smile.

We all chuckled.

"We're going to hear a lot about former lives tonight!" he said.

Jo queried me again. "So—you must be an expert on UFOs."

"Why do you say that?"

"Billy Meier?" she reminded me.

Her smile went straight to my heart. "Oh! Right! No—I'm anything but an expert."

"Have you ever seen a UFO?" she asked.

I didn't have to think about it. I was fine with the truth. "Yes, as a matter of fact. I have. A few."

That caught Rick's attention. "I'm fascinated by this whole topic. What'd you see?"

I explained what I'd seen recently. They were all fascinated, although Jo was familiar with such reports. "Actually, UFO abduction has been a recent field of study of mine," she said. "I'm doing my doctoral dissertation in psychology on that topic. I'm sure you're already aware of it, but you should be careful, Richard. Many of my abductees have reported horrific experiences with the Greys—short, grey creatures with large beady black eyes. They're very scary, very intrusive, doing terrible things to people. I don't find any good coming from most of my abductees' experiences. Some people have described their encounters as terrifying."

"Doesn't anything favorable ever come from contact?" I queried.

"Well, one favorable aspect of the study I'm conducting is that it looks like five percent of the subject population describe wonderful, loving, etheric beings, and the experience rather dramatically changed their lives. But that's rare at only five percent."

Sid probed. "How did it change their lives?"

"Spiritually. It seems to have given them a more conscious life view."

"I've been an amateur UFO buff for years," Rick softly interjected. "It seems there's two extremes out there. I understand that a few well-respected experts in the field believe that our government has struck some kind of deal with aliens. Do you think that's true, Jo?"

"It's been rumored, but there's no way to substantiate it," she said, then turned her attention to me. "Do you think you've had any contact with alien intelligence?"

I took a quick glance at Anoeschka before pensively answering to make sure my sensitive niece didn't jump up and run off confronted with a topic to which I knew she had only been recently introduced. Jo's question brought up all kinds of emotion for me. Revealing I'd seen UFOs in the sky was something countless numbers of people had reported. So what? But contact? With alien intelligence no less? I didn't even know the origin of my own contact. Had it been alien, another dimension or was it something else?

I seemed clear about two things. My interactions from childhood to present time with these higher forms of life were not originating out of an altered state of consciousness. They rose out of an undeniable state of a new reality. My mind hadn't created the telepathic invitation. My mind merely enabled it and received the information. I sensed that to reveal these facts to anyone else might put me in jeopardy of appearing virtually out of my mind. However, I was secure enough in my own sanity and felt almost an obligation to be open about my encounters. Perhaps what little I knew could help someone else, and by sharing, others might offer their observations for my own clearer understanding.

"Yes! I've had contact, but I don't know who or what they are."

Anoeschka stared at me with eyes that I could read—uncertainty over my lack of privity. I was completely surprised at myself at how almost cavalier it came off, never dreaming I'd have revealed such a personal experience to complete strangers. Hearing myself say it actually brought that truth even closer. Sid shifted uncomfortably in his seat and intentionally pressed down hard on my shoe. "But I don't know, actually, what any of this means," I offered. "I mean contact and all."

Two men on my right simultaneously turned in their seats toward me. They had been listening with interest. "Excuse me, but I couldn't help overhearing your discussion," said the young man seated next to me. He looked straight into my eyes. I read his expression perfectly. I could tell he was deeply moved. He extended a handshake to me.

"Hi! I'm Christopher Balazich and this is my co-traveler in time, David Cooper."

We all exchanged further introductions and pleasantries.

"David and I have also established contact," said Christopher.

I was surprised at the coincidence. Christopher's gaze upon me was steadfast and inescapable. He was a handsome young man about six feet tall, swimmer's build, short brown hair, hazel eyes and a very friendly, smiling face. He projected a sense of childlike innocence and curiosity. There was an instant connection between us that seemed to transcend rational explanation—a feeling of familiarity like I had just experienced with Jo. It was all beginning to feel a bit odd.

I wanted to reaffirm what I thought I heard Christopher say. "You did say you also have had contact?" Christopher nodded back, reading my expression. My own experience suddenly felt that much more validated. "Wow. Wow," I muttered under my breath.

Christopher smiled warmly at me. "Who's your contact?"

I was embarrassed. I felt I was being asked as if I should at least know a first name. Thinking about it for a few seconds, I confessed. "I have no idea!"

"Then how do you know it's a contact?" probed Jo.

"I was in my house. I was overcome by a…well…let's say an energy. It said—" I stopped. A grimace shot across my face at the same time Sid nonchalantly stomped gently on my foot again. I caught Sid's eyes and reassured him without a word.

David leaned around Christopher and spoke softly, "They spoke to you?"

"Uh—" I was befuddled. It seemed all too ridiculous coming off my lips.

"It happened to us too," Christopher interjected.

"It did?" I asked without having expected such confirmation.

"Yes!" David said comfortingly.

David was small, wiry and easily had ten years on Christopher's late twenties. He smiled a lot and for some reason reminded me of a court jester. Only later did I learn that David was a yoga master. His high-spirited nature seemed to more than compensate for a physically diminutive stature. He had brown eyes, very dark tan skin, short and slightly curly black hair. His tendency to over articulate dominated his modulated speech pattern.

"So, what did they say to you, Richard?" Rick asked with focused attention.

I swallowed hard, still bewildered by the message I had received. I decided I'd reveal only part of the message with the hope that one of the guests might offer some logical interpretation. "Well, one of the things I heard through a telepathic voice was, you will create a landing base." Shocked that I actually revealed this, there was a short pause of silence.

Jo gasped. "Dear Lord!" she said from somewhere deep inside her. She cleared her throat.

Sid, already privy to the full extraterrestrial invitation, wondered why I was so bold in revealing something so wild.

Scratching his balding head, Rick was equally stumped. "A landing base."

I wasn't sure if Rick was asking a question or confirming what he had just heard me say. He released a nervous laugh and yanked down both sides of his shirt collar.

I had to interject my thoughts. "I know! I know! I haven't the foggiest idea what that means either or how or why I'd even do that. Or even who's asking me! It's strange. It's all really crazy, isn't it?"

Ceiling lights systematically turned off and the stage was being readied.

"I don't think it's so crazy. Christopher and I have communicated with one being. However, our contact doesn't fit Jo's description."

"What's the being's name?" Rick asked.

"He said if light had sound, his name would be Immoway."

I probably looked confused.

David clarified. "It means way of the light."

I still didn't understand.

"So, you've actually seen Immoway?" Jo queried.

"We've been allowed to see him only in the dream state," Christopher said.

It didn't make sense to me. "Then how do you know he's even real?"

"These dreams are more like visions," David explained. "If you ever had one, you'd know. There are no words to describe the experience. It's as real as all of us sitting right here. And what I've seen in my...*dream*," David said, pausing just long enough to flick his two fingers on both hands for air quotes, "Christopher had also seen in his dreams years before we met."

"I think you're referring to lucid dreaming," Jo offered.

"Yes, that's what it is," David confirmed. "It's the place spirit can communicate with us. Three years before I met David, Immoway came to me in this same spiritual state. He foretold of David coming into my life. Even the month! The lucid dreams were guidance for us both by our master teachers."

I didn't understand. "Which master teachers?"

"Oh!" Rick exclaimed. "If you don't know about master teachers, Adele usually begins her talk about them."

"Well, I know a little about them," I stated. "I was just asking which one."

"That's a whole other story," Christopher said.

Jo turned to Christopher. "I'd like to know more about Immoway. Where does he come from?"

"He and his group are pure light beings and they say they operate within our consciousness and therefore communication is quite easy."

"If only we humans allow it to happen," explained David.

"For our own good," Christopher added. "They travel inside of vehicles resembling what many people report being UFOs."

Anoeschka could no longer hold back. "Pardon me, but why would heavenly beings if they are truly sent by our Creator Father still need any type of technology to travel?" I gave Anoeschka another encouraging smile. I too was curious about Christopher's interpretation. She continued. "So, are you saying that's what UFOs are?"

David was quick to respond to the query. "No. That's what some are."

I needed clarification. "Then, where do they come from?"

"Our contact exists within our consciousness," Christopher reaffirmed, although still not satisfactorily answering my question.

Before I could extract more information, a gal from the aisle waved to Rick who stood up and exited the row.

"Are you leaving?" Anoeschka asked.

"Nope! I'm going to be right here with you all."

Rick headed up to the side of the stage, grabbed a microphone then stepped onto the stage. The audience quieted itself and overhead lights dimmed. I turned in my seat and looked around the auditorium. A man behind me sunk down into his chair. The room was packed and people were standing along the sides of the room. I was impressed.

"Good evening everybody. My name is Rick and I'd like to welcome all of you here tonight. Before Adele comes up on stage she asked me to read one of the poems from her book." He proceeded to read a very sweet eight-line verse from one of her poems and then resoundingly introduced her. "And now it's my great pleasure to introduce Mrs. Adele Gerard Tinning!"

The audience fixed their eyes straight on Adele who carefully and slowly took the three steps up the side of the stage and onto the corner landing. The audience applauded with quiet pronouncement.

"Oh Rick! You make it sound so official! You'd think I was going to tap dance for you folks or something," Adele said, embarrassed by the formality of it all.

The audience laughed with Adele and Rick while she walked over to a small drop-leaf wooden kitchen table where two chairs on opposite sides were perpendicular to the audience. She nestled into her seat with her large belly flush against the rim of the table. She stretched her terribly swollen legs straight out, then tucked them back beneath her seat. Her ankles were obviously swollen causing discomfort. As she settled in, she slowly rotated herself in the chair and scanned the audience.

"Hi everyone. I am Adele! God Bless each and every one of you for coming out of your warm and cozy homes to be here tonight. It's really got to be you now doing God's work because I'm not long for this world, dear ones. But enough about me." She adjusted herself more comfortably in her chair, took in a deep breath, released it and again panned the audience. "How are you all doing tonight?"

The audience applauded cautiously and quietly again, not wanting to raise the energy level higher than she might desire. But Adele protested. "Oh, come on now! You've got to be doing better than that! How are you?"

Suddenly everyone responded in uproarious laughter and applause that filled the room. People were heard screaming various accolades, "We love you, Adele!" The room was charged. We were all fully charmed by her charisma.

"Now that's better! I love you, too!" she replied. "My, my! Look at all you beautiful people here tonight. You know, you've all lived many, many times before. Many lives. Hundreds, even thousands. We get to be different races and religions so we can learn those precious lessons necessary for our souls. The Arab who kills a Jew is reincarnated Jewish. A white man who kills a black man comes back black. That's how we learn. We're all equal. God wants it that way.

"Each of us has a guardian angel, a guide from the other side who protects and guides us. It can even be our master teacher. Our challenge is to listen. Sometimes you can hear this guide as a thought or a feeling, a presence, a whisper or even a voice. An angel is always with you, guiding you, directing you to make the best decisions for yourself. When you can live your life in total compliance with your inner voice, you are fully doing God's work. And in

doing so, you bring unconditional love to the world. That's why we're all here, dear ones. *Love and compassion must fill every moment.* That's our task.

"When you die, you cross over to the other side to study what you've done on Earth. And each time you come back, you come back with more understanding and compassion. Now, I don't know how much more the good Lord expects me to be doing in this lifetime. I still have one more reincarnation ahead of me.

"Well, enough about that for now. When you came in tonight you were given a ticket. Rick will randomly pick the other half of your tickets out of the basket up here and when your number is called, please come right up on stage. No applauding please. We want to get to as many people tonight as possible. There's so little time. Please look at your number now."

"Zero-one-two-eight," came Rick's voice.

Immediately a screech of excitement came from one area of the room accompanied by subdued laughter from the audience. A young woman ran up onto the stage and sat opposite Adele at the small table.

"What's your name, dear?"

"Dorothy."

"Have we met before?"

"Not this lifetime!"

The audience laughed with Adele.

"Now place your hands palms down on the table like mine without putting any pressure on the table. Think of someone close to you, dear, within your mind, while I bring in my master teacher Zoro. Silently ask for three numbers or letters that will confirm this is the person you want to be here. Sometimes I have difficulty listening in both worlds at the same time so you must do the counting and remember the responses."

"Okay," Dorothy replied, thinking of three specific letters of the alphabet.

After half a minute, the table began tipping up and over on two of the four legs then back to the floor, each time generating an audible clack echoing across the stage. The first series of eight tips ended with the table flat on all legs representing the eighth letter of the alphabet: H.

"Go on, Zoro," Adele commanded. "Complete her question please."

The table began tipping and tapping again until it tapped out B and D.

"It's the correct initials, Adele. It's H-B-D."

"Oh good. Now ask this spirit one question in your mind."

Dorothy was briefly quiet. "Got it."

The table immediately started tipping up and over on two of the four legs then back down. Dorothy counted off each alphabetical sequence beginning with A. She then put all the letters together. "P-U-D-G-E," Dorothy said.

Adele looked puzzled. "Pudge? What does that mean?"

"Yes," she said tearfully. "Pudge was my daughter's nickname."
"Oh I'm so sorry, dear. She's at the table now. When did she pass?"
"Four years ago."
"What happened?"
"She was hit by a car."
"Oh, honey."
"I miss her so, Adele."
"Of course you do!"

Shock across my face was picked up by Christopher who leaned his head over and whispered, "David and I have been coming here to see Adele for a few years. She's seen over 20,000 people at her residence. She's the real deal."

I felt like I needed that reassurance. I smiled and nodded politely, though I didn't understand the mechanism behind Adele's success at the table. Inside, with a yearning and desperate desire to believe it all, I was indeed hoping she was the real deal.

Ever since the table began moving seemingly of its own accord, Anoeschka had been observing Adele's arthritically knotted finger joints. It was making her uncomfortable. She inched ever closer to me.

"Everybody in the room please be still and control your thoughts," Adele said. "You know, you must always control your thoughts in life. They're so powerful. It's so important not to have random thoughts pass through. The mind is like a filter. It can trap thoughts…thoughts you don't want there. You can't afford to let the mind get all plugged up."

I recalled my childhood experience with the Maharishi Mahesh Yogi. From that one experience alone I had learned the power of thought. However, using the mind at the table with a medium was something new to me. I reflected on my experience with the extraterrestrial invitation, telepathy and the mind, so who was I to doubt anyone?

After Dorothy, a man in his early forties sat with her. He got through two preliminary questions confirming three initials and identity of the person from the other side. One answer Adele's table tapped out was the correct three-digit telephone area code where his friend lived. Adele kicked off both shoes. Her swollen ankles were lost within a fleshy mass.

"What happened to him, honey?"
"Blaze was with me in Vietnam. We were each other's eyes and ears. I owe my life to him, Adele, more than once. I'm indebted to this guy who gave his life for several of us."
"He wants you to know that God also intervened and saved your life. Do you want to ask Blaze one last question?"
"Is he okay?"
"Ask him—one tip of the table is no, two is partly right or doubtful, three

tips are yes."

"You okay, Blaze?" Tears rolled down his face. "They treatin' you okay over there?"

The table immediately tipped three times back and forth on two legs and rested back on the floor.

Adele's eyes were glazed. She closed them, paused and opened them again. "He's okay, honey. God takes care of all of us, dear."

The ex-soldier brushed tears from his face as quickly as Sid. He was so obviously devastated, barely able to move. It was remarkable that a spirit could tap out letters of the alphabet, but having one's hands on the table may have been a factor. I kept reminding myself to remain open. I knew this could be a battle of rethinking and deprogramming my own lifelong conditioning, preconceived notions, ill-conceived reasoning and incorrect understanding, but I was committed to changing these very things.

Many people of all ages and races sat with Adele during the evening, confirming the presence of loved ones by silently asking questions and getting correct answers. Susan was agonizing over the recent loss of her husband. Adele engaged with her.

"It spells *not yet time,* honey."

"I need him, Adele."

"But he's telling you it's not your time. You cannot go before your time, dear."

"I love him, Adele," Susan confessed, tortured by his absence. "I want to be with him."

Adele sensed Susan's inclination to want to pass over. "This is not the way, dear. Tell him you love him. He can hear you."

The table was motionless with all four wooden legs on the floor.

The woman cried to her husband, "I can't bear this without you, Teddy!"

"Dear, tell him you love him."

With feelings of her husband ripped from her heart, she genuinely glared into empty space between her and Adele. "I love you, Teddy. I love you. I love you!"

Suddenly the table gently tipped up and over on two legs and leaned firmly into her and rested against her abdomen. Susan's sense of loss, her pain, suffering and hopelessness were palpable, and yet, deftly balanced against Adele's charm and unconditional love.

"He's hugging you, dear. Can you feel him here with you? He hears you," Adele said with such authority, empathy and command that if his ghost had appeared no one would have been surprised.

"I love you, Teddy!" Susan wailed with tears streaming from her cheeks. "Ohhh, I miss you!"

The edge of the table remained tightly against her mid-section. There was an invisible sense of reassurance that seemed to stem the tide of loss for Susan. I just could not understand how this interaction was occurring. The deepest emotions experienced by Susan were ubiquitous across the room and finally touched me deeply. I sensed that if you didn't feel anything for this heartbroken woman you weren't human despite proving or disproving the presence of any spirit.

I could hear Jo sniffling. From my jacket I retrieved a fresh tissue, leaned forward and handed it to her. She nodded in appreciation. David ran a handkerchief under his nose. Sadness in the room seemed contagious.

"Ask him to touch you somewhere toward the top of your body, honey," Adele suggested. "Anywhere."

The room was silent. Everybody waited and watched, then Susan gasped. "Yes! Yes! He did! Oh Adele! He did!"

A wave of giggling swept the room. There was a sense of relief. Adele's flushed cheeks seemed filled with her smiles. It remained impressive to me that so many people had nailed the correct responses from the questions they silently asked. It required a leap of faith to believe this. This was mind-to-mind, thought-to-thought communication involving loved ones on the other side and master teachers connecting with the living, so I knew this would take some time to digest. Once again, being unfamiliar with Adele, I knew I'd be the first to stand by my own mystical experiences and convictions that could not be rationally explained. So, this required trusting what you could not see or prove.

Finally, Adele sat alone at the table. She was worn out. Her eyes were still glazed. "You see? Thought is so powerful," she said in a very soft, slow and measured voice that usually came from the exhaustion of a marathon. "You know, they're so smart on the other side. Knowledge simply comes to them as it's needed. *It's so important not to condemn another person for what they believe or say or do or think. Do not judge people. We do not know why people do what they do or say what they say. Just forgive them and love them.*"

Adele took in a deep breath and released it. The presentation was over after about twenty people sat with her. The lights came on and a light applause was heard. People started gathering their belongings preparing to leave, but even the guests were ambling in slow motion. The emotional impact from the presentation seemed to be weighing heavily on everyone.

"If you'd like to meet Adele," Christopher offered, "let's go up there. She's a good friend." The group and I slumbered our way to stage-side where Adele was autographing copies of her book. Looking up to the stage I saw the charm of Adele. She had my grandma's shock of hair as white as her fair skin. Her cobalt blue eyes were set in a kind, round face, and her puffy arms with sagging pink skin reminded me of my elder aunts. By observation of her physical presence, I imagined she should have been in a lot of pain, but her alluring smile embedded across rosy cheeks hid any pain she might have been enduring.

Once the crowd around Adele thinned, Christopher and David made the introductions. When I was introduced as an audiologist and published author, Adele perked up. "Do you happen to know Dr. Puharich?"

"No," I immediately confirmed.

"Well, I just met him. Oh, he's so bright," she said. "He's a physician and has patents in the hearing field. But most interesting is that he's been in contact with our space brothers."

"Really?"

"Yes."

"Adele, I'd love to meet him."

"I have his number at home."

She had me. I was all hers from that moment. She laughed from the pit of her belly like an old Buddha, spoke from her heart like a saint, and perpetually felt she hadn't done enough. She seemed genuine and humble, especially not having charged anyone for the presentation or for her books.

Following further chitchat among ourselves, Christopher spotted Adele's swollen ankles. "Adele, you have to take better care of yourself."

"Oh! God will take care of me, honey. Don't you worry about me!"

"Adele, you certainly touch a lot of people," Jo said. "I enjoyed being with you. This was my first time seeing you. You're an amazing woman."

"Oh stop! I'm just a messenger! God's the amazing one, honey! You see how He works? Honey, you could do the same thing. Why don't you all come over to the house tonight? I can give your friend Dr. Puharich's number."

Christopher didn't want to intrude or take advantage of Adele's kindness. "Oh Adele, you're exhausted. Not tonight."

"It's no bother, kids. I've got cakes and pies at the house and somebody brought over some fresh potato salad this morning—"

"Adele, I can always give you a call to get his number," I suggested.

"You rest tonight," David thoughtfully insisted. "We'll bring our new friends over another time."

Despite understanding that Christopher and David were looking out for Adele's best interest, I could tell Jo was disappointed. I was too. "I've got to get back to Los Angeles anyway," Jo said, "and it's a bit of a drive. "Thank you, Adele."

A middle-age woman placed a sweater around Adele's shoulders.

"Oh honey, this body's holding a reserve of heat of its own!" she said, dropping it to the side.

In front of the Scottish Rite Temple, Christopher and David said their good-byes while the rest of us exchanged comments about the evening. Jo turned to me. "I'd love to go to the table with her sometime for a personal session. Wouldn't you?"

I didn't have to think about it. "She's remarkable, although I still love things I can see, taste, touch and measure," I said with a chuckle. "I know many people believe it," I said sheepishly, "but I'm new to this whole thing. I might have to see her again to learn more about channeling."

"Excuse me, Doctor," Jo said with a broad smile and more than a touch of sarcasm, "but aren't you the one who two hours ago said you heard a voice and an extraterrestrial communicated with you? Correct me if I'm mistaken, but isn't that channeling?"

I was struck by the paradox. "I did say a voice, didn't I?"

"Yes. A voice."

This got me laughing at myself along with Anoeschka. "Well yes, that is true," I affirmed.

Jo was laughing too. "It's channeling," she said. "It doesn't mean that you're crazy or you have some kind of disorder or disease or need treatment! If I put on my psychologist's hat, that's my opinion. It's no big deal. You're clairaudient and it sounds like you're also a contactee."

"You know, if she can do this mind to mind, you realize the implications?"

"Of course we do. That's why everyone came here. That's why a hundred and fifty people showed up tonight." Jo warmly smiled at me. "Do _you_ realize the implications?"

I released a laugh from the gut that triggered a chuckle from Jo and Anoeschka. "I know. Do I sound like a complete hypocrite?"

Jo peered directly into my eyes. "Not really. Adele has a gift and if you've never seen her before, it's an awakening. If ever I can be of help in your quest," she said with an inviting smile, "please call me."

"Thank you! And may I ask? I don't see a ring on your finger." I raised my eyebrows.

"Uncle Richard!" Anoeschka spontaneously blurted out in a near reprimand, holding her face in a failed attempt to hide more blushing.

"Hmmm. You put it right out there, don't you?" Jo teased. "I don't usually mix business with pleasure," she qualified with my kind of sarcasm.

Anoeschka's deeply conservative ways were creating far too much discomfort. "Okay! I'll see you at the car Uncle Richard! Nice to meet you, Jo."

"My pleasure Anoeschka," Jo replied with a warm embrace. "So lovely chatting with you."

Sid handed Anoeschka the car keys as I moved closer to Jo and whispered, "By the way who said anything about business?"

She couldn't help herself from chuckling and appreciating my boldness.

"I'm divorced," she said with a smile, still gazing into my eyes. "Should you ever want company when you meet with Dr. Puharich, I'd be happy to serve lunch."

"Hey, that's a deal!"

After we exchanged numbers, Jo walked away. I couldn't help gawking at the way she moved her slender body down the sidewalk. Continuing to walk backwards beside Sid with my focus straight on her, I said, "I like psychology!"

Sid lit up a cigarette. "Look, I don't mean to interrupt your sex life or anything," he said. He took a few quick puffs. "Now what's your opinion of her?"

Walking backwards still ogling at Jo as she was almost out of sight, I declared in a loving tone, "What a woman!"

"See! I told you you'd love Adele."

"I mean Jo!"

With a huge clatter the back of my head smacked into a large No Parking sign.

Sid burst out laughing. "See! God's sending you a message! Listen up!"

CHAPTER ELEVEN

Although I had been talking with Jo only by telephone for a couple weeks, after work one day I walked into the bedroom and flicked on the overhead light. In an effort to draw into consciousness and eventually into reality the presence of my potential life partner, I had created and hung a dream board above my bed. Pasted dead center among countless artful magazine cutouts, photos and gorgeous greeting card images was an artist's inked sketch of an angelic female figure. Her tornado of dark chocolate hair was a thicket of dangles which encompassed endlessly long curls that fell far below her shoulders. It was the symbolic image of the very angel I was hoping to meet one day. It was Jo.

I was glued to this moment with rapt attention. I moved closer to view this heavenly image which I had added to the board only a few months earlier. I was surprised that I had failed to observe this hanging right above me every night when I went to bed. I took it as a reminder of the need to be more mindful. I closed my eyes and gave my deepest thanks to the universe for whatever force made this gift possible. While I knew I was terribly vulnerable, I also knew I had to keep my heart open. Balancing a potential budding romance with my single-minded mission might prove to be quite the juggling act.

After a quick wash I headed out for a light dinner. When I entered the Good Earth Restaurant the hostess seated me. Sitting a good five minutes without attention, I flagged down a busboy to finally get a glass of water to quench my thirst. There were relatively few customers in the restaurant so I couldn't understand the delay. Finally, a waitress came over. I ordered a large bowl of soup, a side salad with poppyseed dressing and an iced herbal tea with no ice.

I could tell the waitress preferred not to be working that night. It was her tone of voice. She was quick with her questions and short with her patience. When the soup arrived, the bowl was half filled—about a cup's worth. After she set it down, I politely asked if she wouldn't mind if I was to have a bit more soup in the bowl, explaining why. She grabbed the bowl quickly, sloshing soup out and over into the dish beneath it and marched off. The only edibles on the table were two rolls. I reached for one. Instead of the usual soft and heated rolls, they were hard and room temperature. In a few moments the waitress returned with the soup bowl full. Once she set it down, I politely explained the issue with the rolls.

She squinted her eyes to a near slit, puckered her lips and just stood there looking through me for a fraction of a second, but long enough to make her point. If she had gritted her teeth any tighter, I was certain she'd have cracked a molar. Saying nothing, she removed the rolls.

The tea and salad were delivered, but I immediately caught the error.

"Ma'am, this looks like herbal dressing on the salad. I actually wanted herbal tea and poppyseed dressing."

"Sir, I wrote down herbal dressing," she said emphatically.

"Yes. I'm sure you did."

She let out a sigh of frustration and removed the salad. I was sure Murphy's Law was in full swing. At this point the only things I had on the table were the bowl of soup, an empty water glass waiting for a refill, no warm rolls and no herbal tea. I got thinking how bad days are like a disease. You can pick it up from anybody if you're not careful. I was determined not to let her attitude ruin my evening.

The salad was returned with the proper dressing and I purposely did not ask for the herbal tea thinking I might be shot dead before I'd ever make it to the exit door. Long finished with the soup, the hot rolls arrived. I decided I was lucky. However, it also felt like survival of the fittest. I needed my herbal tea.

"Excuse me ma'am," I said, afraid to say anymore, pointing to my empty herbal tea glass and smiling.

The tea arrived with such speed that I had to look up to believe it was the same waitress. But it was. She was grinning. While eating the salad, I mulled over the events with the waitress. The more I thought about the situation, the angrier I found I was getting. I felt justified. The service used to be excellent. I couldn't figure out how I ran into such bad luck. Replaying the complete lack of hospitality she had demonstrated in our short encounter, I found myself thinking how she's paid to perform a service and her service wasn't worth a wooden nickel. Finishing the last morsels of the salad and while the ice tea glass had remained empty for too long, I strategized how I might go about letting her know of my displeasure.

Report her to the manager? No. That's not good enough, I imagined. *Leave her one penny tip?* Too weak I countered. *No tip whatsoever?* No. *Confront her with the truth about why she deserves absolutely no tip?*

While wrestling with various tactics that would unfortunately inflame an already irritated woman, something likened to a vortex seemed to slowly open within me. Sitting quietly in my seat, a Voice came out of nowhere.

"You are why the world does not have love."

I looked around. No one was there. I was astonished. This was remarkable. I was certain my mind had to be playing tricks on me so I ignored it. My thoughts returned to the lesson I would teach the waitress. And again, a bit more firmly the Voice whispered. ***"You are why the world does not have love."***

The Voice was unmistakable in its diction. It was a male voice and adamant in its tone. It seemed like it could certainly be the echo of my conscience, but it was in the form of an actual audible vocalization, one that the conscience itself cannot make audible. I never conversed with a voice like this. Illogical as it may seem, I thought it could even be a trick by a voice emanating out of a speaker on the wall. I wasn't even certain who this voice was addressing.

"Me?" I whispered in complete bewilderment.

"You," the Voice replied. *"And you should leave her a good tip."*

Astonished, I blurted out, "No! She deserves nothing!" I was so quick with my pronouncement that I was embarrassed by such a kneejerk reaction. While completely beguiled by this interaction, I was still stubborn in my position.

"No!"

"This is why the world does not have love," returned the Voice.

"What?" I questioned, befuddled, not believing my own ears.

"You are part of the world and you do not give love."

"But she isn't giving me love," I said in a hasty schoolboy response.

"She is not of whom I speak."

I was overcome by the depth of this interchange. Either my higher self had suddenly become audible, or just as mysteriously, I was hearing a Voice originating from somewhere else. Audibility of this Voice was unmistakable.

"How do I give love to someone who isn't loving?" I sheepishly queried.

"By giving love," spoke the Voice. *"From where must love come if not from within you? And from where must fear and anger stop if not from within you?"*

I was overcome with chills. I almost could not believe what was happening. I recognized that I could not now turn away from the very truth in which I was confronted. Although the Voice held a certain firm tone, I saw past the reprimand to the wisdom in the message. However, my need to 'enlighten' the waitress was ever-pressing. With a parched throat from the tension, I stared at the empty glasses of water and herbal tea yet to be replenished. The waitress was nowhere to be seen. I went over and over how I was going to give love to a woman for whom distain within me weighed heavier than kindness. Despite the greater sense of wisdom from the Voice now echoing in my head, on the scale of justice, I only saw reckoning. No tip!

The Voice was even firmer. *"Not only should you leave her a good tip, but two times a good tip."*

My mind was locked on poor service. "I can't do that!"

When I stood up and placed less than double a good tip on the table, I heard, *"Please sit down."* The Voice was so adamant that I again turned around to look expecting someone to be standing there. I was still alone. I sat back down —flabbergasted. This was some kind of projection, telepathy or thought transference. I knew somebody was reading my mind, maybe even my heart. However, I was more inclined to dismiss it than accept it, despite what I had witnessed with Adele's interactions.

"You cannot leave the table like this, for you have not left her with love. You have only left her with money."

I was simply stupefied by this challenge. "Oh, come on," I answered reflexively. "I can't do that! You don't know how it works here," I insisted. "I just can't do that!"

While I sat quietly contemplating the drama with this Voice, I was suddenly struck by the reality of what I was doing to myself. Despite how loving I thought I was, I just could not give love to this woman. It just didn't fit into the equation of events that had transpired around such lousy service.

With whispered gentility the Voice again spoke. *"You are why the world does not have love."*

While I was thinking about just walking out, I was far too curious about this mysterious interaction. Two times a tip is one thing but *with love?* I was at an impasse. I pondered this idea and in a moment of introspection I recognized the futility of my stubbornness. I saw what I was doing to myself. I recognized my ignorance and foolishness. However, I didn't yet understand that all I needed to do was emotionally detach myself from the situation, open my heart, feel the pain in which this woman was trapped and show true compassion. Then I could give her all the love she needed. And she needed it. She was broken in this world because of her own drama and traumatizing events that had ensnared her life. What she needed was as much love from as many people as there were to open their hearts to her, before she took her own life. But I was fixated on poor service, justification and rationalization that would make her evening even worse.

I stood up and left the table with additional gratuity, but no extension of love to a poor soul in distress. I could not surmount my aggravation in order to open my heart. On the way to my car, ruminating over my attitude, I was humiliated by my action and reactions. How could I have been given wisdom of mercy and elected not to reach out to a suffering sister on the planet? Was she any different than me? I was caught in a conundrum wherein I saw the logic of a comforting action I could have put forth but declined. It could have been a question about how her evening was going. Or a kind word that might have changed her mood. Maybe a nod of my head would have hinted that I understood her pain. The crack of a smile could have conveyed she wasn't so alone. But I could not get out of my own way. Deep inside I knew my actions ran counter to any claim of being a loving person let alone one who thought of himself as spiritual.

By the time I was sitting in the car I was battered by my own shame. Keeping the mind open to all things possible was only half the journey. I had left my heart behind. I realized that if the shift to love cannot start with every single person taking complete responsibility at every opportunity that comes along and separating oneself from someone else's issues, miseries, pain and drama that reflect poorly onto others, how will this world ever change?

I recalled Adele's wisdom. I thought I had it cemented in my mind, but apparently it had not yet carved its way to my heart. *It's so important not to condemn another person for what they believe or say or do or think. Do not judge people. We do not know why people do what they do or say what they say. Just forgive them and love them.*

What possible benefit was there to feelings of revenge or being insensitive to another person? What was I doing to myself with all these emotions that did nothing but hinder growth? Still sitting behind the wheel, I did forgive the waitress. I even extended love to her. But there was a much deeper place I had to go if I was to really be honest with myself and rise above my own inadequacies. I had to forgive *myself.* This was a higher hurdle than forgiving others because it forces acknowledgment of your shortcomings. For an obsessive-compulsive perfectionist, recognizing myself as so imperfect turned out to be not just an awakening, but a cathartic cleansing because it was an opportunity to address it. It was an opportunity for change.

CHAPTER TWELVE

Arriving at the clinic Jim Stanton queried me about the current data collection. We engaged in a short discussion about my progress when the conversation turned to the very topic I had been hoping to avoid.

"Dion tells me you've been seeing some things in the sky. True?" Jim asked with an odd smile.

Hesitant to answer honestly but knowing no other way to respond, from my computer station I haltingly raised my eyes to Jim. "True."

"UFOs?"

"Well, some call them UFOs. Unknown craft in the sky for sure."

"Come on."

There was no way that I was going to subject myself to ridicule and share with him that I had received a telepathic message inviting me to Palm Springs. "Hey, you're asking me to explain something about which I have nothing more than a visual sighting and something I myself don't yet fully understand."

"Exactly! This is why people jump to calling things something they aren't. You're probably seeing airplanes or—"

"Jim, airplanes don't stop dead in the air and hover."

"Helicopters do."

"Without a sound?"

"You bet, depending on how far away you are." He didn't pause long enough to even consider the notion. "I'm sure it's explainable. There's never been a shred of evidence left behind by a UFO."

"What are you saying? Therefore, they don't exist? That's inverse logic."

He persisted. "But if they're real as kooks claim, we'd have hard evidence by now, wouldn't we? You don't really believe that an alien species could figure out the barriers to time and space, come to Earth, and then not reveal themselves? Does that make any sense? For what purpose? And why do they always seem to contact farmers in rural areas instead of going directly to the President in Washington or to scientists?"

I looked at Jim who for a second seemed caught in his own paradox.

"Scientists?" I asked with a smirk then a smile.

The conversation was interrupted when Doris came over and handed me an audiogram on a patient waiting in a treatment room. I headed over.

I was met by a tall sixty-year-old gentleman. His hand was extended. He was gleaming.

"Good morning, Mr. McAlister. I'm Richard."

"Hi Doc, what a pleasure to meet you, sir."

We exchanged a handshake and I cordially invited him to have a seat. He was a handsome man about as tall as me. His tan skin was pleasantly contrasted against his graying brown hair. He had well-defined features and an elongated face with a prominent carved jawline. Before I could begin an interview or delve into his case history, my young spirited new patient stopped me.

"Doc, I must tell you the strangest thing. You'll see from the case history I just filled out I've been suffering with this unrelenting full feeling in my ears for weeks. That's what motivated me to finally come see you. When I parked my car in your lot out there, you're not going to believe this, but for the very first time since I had this crazy thing going on, it cleared up! So when I walked into this office, I could hear well."

"Hearing issues can be intermittent or even spontaneously recover. But it is unusual that you'd have it for weeks and suddenly it's gone on this very day."

"Exactly! That's what I'm saying, Doc. It's been plaguing me and been terribly annoying."

"Your audiogram performed today looks pretty normal except for some mild high frequency loss. We can keep an eye on this." I observed a small gold pin with a raised blue cross on it angled into his brown tweed sport coat lapel. I pointed at it. "Are you in the ministry?"

"I've been a pastor for more years than I can count, Doc," he said proudly, pressing his tie against a perfectly ironed shirt.

"I'm sorry. I should be addressing you as Pastor."

"No, no, no. I don't stand on formality. I know who I am. Most people call me Pastor Jack anyway."

"How long have you been in the ministry?"

"My whole life essentially. Since I was a young man," he said in his kind uplifting manner.

I put the folder down on a table and reached for a clipboard. "I just need you to sign a form here." While he signed, I studied him. "May I ask you a personal question since you're in the ministry?"

He set down the pen and clipboard and looked warmly back at me with a broad and embracing smile. "Certainly."

"Even at the risk of jumping off a cliff?"

"No one's ever died asking me a question."

We joined in a good laugh.

The Pastor clasped his hands together on his lap prepared for the challenge.

"Do you ever question the existence of God?"

The question didn't faze the Pastor. I was surprised. "Never! Need you ask a pastor that question?"

"Sorry, but how do you know God exists?"

He looked deeply into me. He could see I was sincere—a searching man. "I see the invisible presence of God all around me. You're a man who thinks for himself. Mathematically something cannot come from nothing, can it?"

"True."

"Then isn't it more reasonable to believe that we've come from an ultra-magnificent creator of infinite love, intelligence and wisdom that we call God than it is to believe that we originated from nothing which in itself is virtually impossible?"

I stopped and thought about what he had reasoned. He was beautifully articulate and I respected his intelligence and sophic position on the matter, but he hadn't addressed a more fundamental issue.

"Yes, I agree in the logic and even in the wisdom and idealism of such a belief, but it still remains only a belief, doesn't it?"

"Does it?"

"Well, I mean, there's no proof. No evidence. I'd be concerned that in the end I'd be a fool to believe in something that doesn't exist."

Some might have been insulted by the comment, but not Pastor Jack. He understood my probing which some might have interpreted as an unbeliever, but he recognized a man in search of truth.

"I have a feeling you're being the devil's advocate," he submitted. "Right?"

"Maybe."

"Is it folly to believe what's in the heart? Is it the fool who says what's in my heart is not real because I can't prove it to you? What's in my heart is more real to me than this desk." He firmly knocked on it. "More real than this cane," he said with a pause, grabbing his tall oak cane and bouncing it hard on the floor a couple times. "What's in my heart is—" he paused again, then pointed his finger straight at me and smiled warmly. "What's in my heart, Doc, is even more real than you."

What a concept. That thought brought a smile to me also. There was an inner peace and tranquility about this good man, a centeredness that seemed to speak true to his convictions. I readily recognized that. It touched me deeply.

"Sometimes, Pastor, I'm not even sure what's in my heart," I confessed.

"Then how can you know what's real in someone else's heart if you cannot see it in your own?"

I was a bit stymied. I nodded and smiled at him again. "You're right."

"I wonder if you wouldn't mind very much helping me to my car," he kindly asked.

"Certainly. But we need to go over your audiogram."

He placed his oak cane in his left hand and stood straight up. "No. We'll go over your question on the way to my car."

We both chuckled again.

"I appreciate you sharing your ideas with me, Pastor."

We walked out into the main clinic through the hub of activity.

"Pardon me, Richard," Doris politely interrupted. "You have a call on line two."

"Please take a message for me. I'll be right back."

"Sorry, Pastor," I said apologetically.

"No, no, I'm sorry if I'm taking you away from your work, Doc."

"No problem, Pastor, this is important to me. I'm very interested in what you have to say. We were talking about the heart."

"Yes. I tell my students if you have heart troubles not of the vascular type," he proffered with a smile, "look back to the last time a relationship didn't work and search for the lessons waiting to be discovered. Then, give it all over to God."

I immediately thought of Annie. "I certainly remember the last relationship well."

"You don't have to reveal it to me so long as you recognize the issues for yourself."

"That's okay. I can tell you. She was an alcoholic woman I was mad about. Loved her with all my heart, but my desire to love and trust were shattered." I swallowed hard. "It's been challenging to even want to engage in a new relationship."

"I understand," he said with real compassion.

"Out of this adversity, Pastor, came a low so low. I felt I wasn't good enough for anyone. I think a part of me almost gave up on myself. I knew my life had to change, so I've been rebuilding it since then."

He crossed the cane over to his other hand and held it while he gently patted me on the back of my hand. "There's no escape from suffering that comes our way. It's woven into the fabric of life. While we might never be able to fully insulate ourselves from it, we're in charge of what we do with it when it's at our doorstep."

"Yes. Yes indeed. You talk like a Buddhist, Pastor. I've been finding that life is a process that battles suffering with a fine line between the laughter and the pain."

"The line's an illusion. It's all but a single process woven into the fabric of living. It's what we do with suffering that matters."

Nodding in agreement we exchanged another warm smile.

In this moment I reflected on our shared wisdom; yet I knew I was trapped in my struggle juggling loneliness, a sexual drive and my relentless pursuit of spirit. I recalled my commitment to Annie. The depth of love. The laughter and high times and my desire for marriage and children. I thought I had found my partner and in an instant the dream and seemingly an important part of my future was catapulted out of my life. It didn't matter that my girlfriend cheated on me. It didn't matter if someone's life had been traumatized by events outside their control. I saw Pastor Jack's point. It's all a single process on a continuum toward doing the best you can. All that matters is what you do with the experiences. I recognized my challenge.

"Pastor, for years I believed that experiencing suffering as a conscious process would eventually release it. You know, the mindful way of Buddha."

My searching eyes and expression must have spoken to him. "Has it, young man? Or does suffering hold you hostage?"

I was pensive. "Maybe I just failed at learning the seven steps to awaken."

"I tell my students you need to go the last step," he said. "Put it in God's hands. He can take the burden. It vanishes once you give it to God. We each have our own path. Your girlfriend had hers too, but in a way, you've taken on her challenges. Give it all to God. That will clear your heart and relieve the suffering. God can handle all the pain and suffering in the world."

"Yes. God. That's the challenge. Hinduism holds to the belief in one Supreme Being who has given life to other gods, somewhat like the Judeo-Christian position of a single God. And Hinduism seems to be based on little religious dogma. On the other hand, in Buddhism there's no single God but many gods. God is in everything, is everywhere and nowhere. In the process of it all, I'm caught in the struggle of the whole notion of God. How can I give my heart and soul to a source that may not even exist? Or as different doctrines tell us, God is found here, there or by this or that belief?"

Pastor Jack looked at me with somewhat forlorn eyes. "You can't, son. You can't. That's the paradox of God. You cannot reap the benefits He holds for you without fundamentally believing in Him. Believe in Him and you'll find Him. That's where people get stuck. Faith is the cornerstone to believing. Are you a member of a local church?"

"I've never been religious. Work's my religion."

"Work will never provide you with spiritual salvation, Doc. The world is in dastardly shape. It's calling for change and for a leader, but there is no earthly leader who can bring us out of the turmoil we're in. We all need salvation."

We reached the end of a hallway where I opened the exit door. The bright sunlight poured down upon us. Pastor Jack put on his sunglasses as rays of sunlight shone down upon him. I escorted him over to his car where he retrieved something from a briefcase, then cradled it against his chest hidden within his folded arms.

"Ever read the Bible?"

I laughed. "Both Old and New Testaments as a scientist, not as a believer."

"Didn't think so!" the Pastor confirmed. We both laughed at the obvious. "Decades ago I started the World Literature Crusade. If I piled up all the literature we sent out, it'd be over a mile high." He extended the New Testament to me. "Please take this. It isn't religion. It goes deeper than that to the written word of God. I want you to have it. This is my own personal Bible. Look—" He opened the cover. "My name is even in it."

"Oh come on now. I've got Bibles and so many books and projects going."

"Please! Allow me. In it you'll find more knowledge than one man could ever hope to comprehend in a lifetime. You're a man who judges things for himself. You can appreciate this. Come on, take it. I've been hoping I'd find someone worthy of receiving it. Just knowing you have it will bring great comfort to me, Doc."

How could I have possibly rejected such kindness? I graciously accepted it out of courtesy and with sincere appreciation for such a thoughtful gesture. "Thank you, Pastor Jack."

He shook my hand and without letting go he pulled me to his chest, tightly, and embraced me. I sensed the purest heart in this gentle man.

After he got in the car, he cranked down the window. "You know young man, I think God sent me to you!" He started the engine without losing a moment's gaze on me. "That terrible blocked feeling for so long, you know? And it mysteriously disappears on this very day, the very day I meet you when you ask me these important questions? I think God sent me to you for reasons perhaps we don't understand right now. I don't think I'll ever have that hearing problem back again."

"I sure hope not, Pastor."

He backed out and threw an almost saluting warm wave. When he drove to the far corner of the lot and started the turn, he looked back at me with my arms cradling the Bible to my chest. I'm certain that brought another smile to his face. He waved back at me.

Returning to the clinic I headed to my desk and thought about my encounter with the Pastor. In moments of meditation I had learned to release the deepest emotions. I sensed I would now have to go deeper into my heart to heal the wounds that could pose a risk of destroying my bourgeoning relationship with Jo. I knew the Pastor was right. Give it all over to God. Yet, there remained just enough uncertainty about God which still made it difficult for me to hold such a view in the heart. That was the enigma.

While I had the highest respect for Pastor Jack, I reflected on my personal biblical studies that had revealed significant discrepancies and Bible inconsistencies in both the Old and New Testaments. These were things with which I certainly did not want to challenge the Pastor. I had come to view biblical text more as historical documents than religious doctrine. I recalled Psalm 145:18, *God is near to all who call on him,* but Psalm 10:1 stated, *God is far away and cannot be found in times of need.* Genesis 1:24-26 read, *Animals were created before man,* but Genesis 2:19 stated, *Animals were created after man.* Genesis 1:31 said, *God was pleased with his creation,* but Genesis 6:6 stated, *God was not pleased with His creation.* Genesis 32:30 said, *For I have seen God face to face and my life is preserved,* but John 1:18 read, *No man hath seen God at any time.* With respect to a moral code of living, while any consideration of slavery today would be incomprehensible, Exodus 21:26-27 indicated slavery was acceptable, *If a master injures his slave, that slave is to go free.*

Man's inhumanity to man and particularly the cruelty to, and dismissal of women that I found in biblical verses, had influenced me in reasoning that moral codes from thousands of years ago were never intended for application to our present-day era. In Deuteronomy 22:20-21 it stated, *If the tokens of virginity be not found for the damsel, then stone her with stones that she die.* We're not going to stone to death anyone even if indicated in any Bible. I recalled other merciless passages for the weak according to verses with which I was familiar. If there was any deformity a person suffered, from a broken foot, blindness, a blemish or even hearing loss, Leviticus 21:18-21 stated, *he or she shall not come nigh to offer the bread of his God.*

These miserably disheartening contradictions ricocheted through me. I was swimming in uncertainty. Surely, we cannot take the Bible literally and thereby be compelled by religious obligation to start stoning people. Certainly, we're not going to reintroduce slavery because in ancient times that was the custom. Nor are we to cherry-pick biblical verses that best suit our hopes and wishes while discounting other verses wherein people find salvation. I knew many people who had discarded the Bible altogether as a relic of barbarism filled with contradictions never intended for future generations.

I always felt in many respects that the Bible could have been a divinely inspired work; yet, through its many edits, manipulations and translations across millennia, almost certainly some Higher Truths had slipped away or were purposely buried. While I wasn't yet even sure where I stood, from my childhood encounter I knew there was so much more to be discovered.

I closed my eyes, listened to my breathing and quieted my thoughts. I wondered if in this lifetime I'd ever find my pathway to the Divine.

CHAPTER THIRTEEN

One evening thinking about Annie, I realized I had to let go of the emotions associated with her. I was being held hostage—too much thinking about my past. I had entirely misjudged her. I made false assumptions of who I thought she was instead of seeing who she really was. She had no self-respect. No dignity. She lacked honor and trustworthiness. The obvious cues I had been willing to overlook had been glaring indicators that screamed at me, telling me to get out as fast as I could. I ignored all the warning signs. Now the failed relationship was beginning to look more like a hidden blessing. However, the remaining damage I was left holding was like chewing on gritty dust. Anger. Bitterness. Betrayals. Most troubling were my own misjudgments of character. None of it was serving a productive purpose. Recognizing that I was the creator of my own suffering, I was ready to give it up. I knew exactly how I'd do it.

In the 1970s, Dion and I conducted effective human studies research with long-term tinnitus sufferers. Our research principle rested in the power of the mind—the power of thought—through guided meditations. We postulated that subjects would be aware of the unwanted noxious stimulus (tinnitus), but have it trigger a relaxation response instead of an anxiety response. The idea behind the study was integrating progressive relaxation, affirmations, and the power of visual imagery and positive thinking in daily living.

As I sat on the living room carpet, I applied a similar principle in order to remedy my unhealthy emotions associated with Annie. I was taking thoughts, in this case bad memories, and transforming them. I began to visualize letting go of all negative emotions. I sat quietly, feeling the anger, the disappointment and sadness. I took in deep breaths, blew them out and kept letting it all go. My goal was to do exactly what Pastor Jack had suggested. I was preparing to give it all over to God even though my concept of God remained vague.

I closed my eyes and began shoveling it all into a bucket. This took some time. There were many shovelfuls. I visualized an open space in the shape of loving arms reaching out to me. I relaxed and really got into the imagination of it. I then sealed it with forgiveness and put a bow on top. I blessed it. I forgave Annie. And I forgave myself which was even more challenging. Perhaps it was Gandhi who said *forgiveness is holiness.*

After concentration that lasted some time, I fired it into open space to God. The bucket was gone. My long sigh was the indicator of my success. Like Adele, the Maharishi, Norman Vincent Peale and countless others have said, *thought is powerful.* BUT—was my vanquishing of emotions more a psychological release than anything else? Was it God that received my release; was it the universe; or was no one there to receive it?

Regardless of an answer, I felt better. I would repeat it as often as needed. This seemed to free me up with a sense of being more emotionally available to Jo. She and I began rocketing forward in a relationship. Our days were filled with hours of telephone conversations. We finally set up a dinner date.

In the meantime, my focus was on the clandestine October 20th invitation to Palm Springs which felt like it was closing in on me even though it was still many weeks away. I was getting nervous. I realized that I had no idea what I was getting into. If this encounter was friendly, that was one thing. I knew I'd be safe. But if they were the Greys like Jo had indicated, there'd be no telling the outcome with even more fear embedded in the anticipation. The most fundamental of questions was ever pressing. Why was I invited to come <u>alone</u>?

Sitting at my desk I closed my eyes, buried my face in my hands and ever so slowly and deeply massaged my face and temples. I searched for the silence between the thoughts that quiets the mind. I began an old Sanskrit mantra. *Aum mane padme hum. Aum mane padme hum.* I repeated this continuously until I locked onto the single syllable Aum, drawing the syllable out until my breath ended, then repeated it continuously. My very long, slow and rhythmic vocalizations of Aum filled my ears until my voice finally went silent. The room was quiet. My consciousness moved to the indwelling sound of the body and soon I was in the deepest state of alpha meditation—almost falling asleep.

When I came out of it, I opened my eyes and looked up from my desk at my study data spread out. I was instantly struck with a feeling that I was not alone. I turned around expecting to find that Sid had snuck in, but nobody was there. My sixth sense was fired up. My eyes scanned the library like I had done only recently when I received the invitation. I turned back around and stared at the drawn curtains over the desk. I reached up and impulsively lurched them apart and glanced into the sky. Three huge stars many times larger and brighter than anything I'd seen yet shimmered in the darkness. I instinctively grabbed a flashlight and ran outside.

The lights were in the formation of three points of a triangle. They glistened with prismatic spinning colors of red, orange, yellow, green and blue which I'd seen before, but far bigger, many times larger than Venus or Jupiter at their brightest. Then, two lights veered off and faded into the night sky. Only a single point of light remained in the northeastern view and progressively moved through the sky toward me. I raised my flashlight and codified a light signal— two followed by three quick flashes. With the flashlight slightly trembling in my hand, I repeated the signal a few times. The vessel continued forward. Frozen in awe I could finally see a shimmering vessel lined with brightly multicolored lights that seemed to rotate clockwise around the middle. I was entranced. I tried to observe objectively, but it was too dark to see much. It appeared close enough to estimate the diameter to be maybe thirty feet across at perhaps a few hundred yards away hovering above rooftops. The lack of reference points made any accurate judgment on size or distance impossible.

Then, all the lights on the vessel went off and two bright headlights came on shining down directly at the trees. I was mystified. While the vessel remained at a fixed altitude it rotated around and slowly flew away. If anyone had viewed this action, I knew it would have been indistinguishable from a common helicopter or small plane in the night sky; and yet in its silence it was anything but common. I didn't know what to make of it.

I ran back into the house to the library and picked up a dictionary. I looked up 'vessel,' not even sure why. There were a few different meanings, but one biblical interpretation jumped off the page: *the repository of some spirit or influence.* Somehow, some way, that idea resonated with me, not about that evening's sighting, but others I'd seen. The qualified description of vessel rather than UFO or craft or ship aptly captured what I inexplicably felt at a much deeper level—almost like family.

Suddenly, in a very strange way that was unexplainable, I felt like I had to lay down or I would fall asleep standing up. I had never quite had this feeling before. There was much more work to get done that evening, but I decided to go into the bedroom for a nap and return to get a few more hours of work done. I laid down on top of the covers. Sleep overtook my consciousness like the infusion of a heavy drug. I was out in seconds.

I found myself in a large classroom with a few other students. It was very strange because in a way I felt like I was still awake. Students were seated in elevated plateau-style rows like a college classroom. I was alone in the middle. A Figure completely shrouded in a thin, beige linen cloth held a wooden pointer to a graph on the chalkboard, one lost among a myriad of other calculations, formulae, symbols and pictographic images scribed across it. I was fascinated. I observed what could have been hundreds of graphic images. I didn't understand any of them—except one at the tip of the pointer. It was a progressively rising audiometric curve, one I sensed I would need to include for analysis in an ongoing study.

Once the awareness of this new environment sunk in, I realized I'd been holding my breath. The sound of air escaping my chest filled my head with resonance. A captivating and bright golden glow emanated from the Figure's head and shroud as he turned to speak. Golden rays obscured clarity of his face.

"Spirit materializes change in the world by movement of space. This is done through you and by your choice," he said in a commanding and all-consuming voice. His words were filled with passion. It also sounded like he was speaking within my head. I understood the message. We can fulfill responsibilities in this world on behalf of a higher order. Spiritual influences can guide us to make wise choices in the world's best interest or in our best interest.

The Figure spoke again. "Remember—space comes from Light, and Light is always guided by the love of God." I understood this to be suggesting that space in the universe comes from Divine Intelligence down through the human spirit. It is Divine Intelligence within us that guides this Light. I understood that while this Light is everlasting, when we remain spiritually mindful, this Light shines brightly through us. It may not be seen, but it will be felt.

He continued. "Spirit can work within coincidence which is our way of reminding you we are with you. This element is Divinely inspired to better serve mankind." I knew I had experienced baffling coincidences that seemed beyond the probability of chance. Was this what he meant? I saw that such influences could come from a higher source with the hope of stoking our awareness to see the unseen. I was beginning to understand that this must be the God Force within us, to be recognized and honored as such.

My mind was reeling. Perplexed and overwhelmed by this extraordinary information, I released a sigh—"Aaaaaaaahhh." The shrouded Figure turned in my general direction. His intense golden light was everywhere.

"To master Light, you must master thought. When you learn the timing and relationship between thought and action, you will see through the window of Divinity to all the Sacred Truths. That's how Divine action occurs. Through thought. Through you. Living this wisdom will unveil lines of synchronicity that shall unfold patterns to you, such that you may even foretell that which is to come."

I understood that you must be master of your thoughts. Such mastery requires skillful self-control of what thoughts we choose to think. I reflected on how meditation achieves this. It quiets random noise in the head in order to capture inner guidance through the simplicity of quiet inner listening. This is the path to mastery. Thoughts are then woven into actions in the world inspired by Spirit. In essence, this is *doing the work of God.*

I understood that lines of synchronicity are merely links between the invisibility of thoughts and the physical manifestations of their corresponding actions in the world. When this is achieved, one is in perfect harmony. I knew if I could listen attentively to the Inner Truths and resonate with them, this must be the Divine process. That is, it's *humans doing God's work.* The more often I could listen and resonate with Higher Truths, the closer I knew I might come to synchronizing my life with a sacred plan. This would be the window into Divinity. Thought and action are so integrally linked that the future seemed indeed predictable because everyone, based on thought alone, is in the process of creating their present and future lives after having already created past lives.

The Figure slowly turned and looked directly at me. A brilliant glow emanated from around his head like fingers of sunlight moving toward me. My connection intensified. From my seat I stared into the shroud trying to gain a greater depth of understanding.

He spoke. *"Imagine a world with no hatred or war. Imagine a world without need. Imagine a world not based on beliefs but attuned to truth, hope, love, charity, faith and healing. Imagine a world where the only religion is Truth from within doing work of the same God for all mankind. Imagine a world where dreams are real. This is the world that is here. These miracles have always been available."*

I had a deep sense of Divine Intelligence coming through this wisdom. That is, a Source that rises within oneself. I understood this as distinctly independent of Off-Planet Intelligence sourced by extraterrestrial contact.

In a single motion the classroom catapulted away from me disappearing into blackness. Just as quickly I awakened. I could remember every detail of the dreamscape including my connection to this Being of Light.

I sat up quickly. Floating a foot in front of my face were two entirely separate, vivid, holographic images side by side. I was shocked. On the left was an old rusted wire coat hanger bent into a single ring at one end and a coiled-like spring at the other. A small square metallic object hung from the ring. I'd never seen anything like it.

The other image on the right was a remarkably sophisticated and complex electronic piece of wizardry I had also never seen. It was computer-like with a few colorful flickering lights, odd switches and controls, an illuminated panel and two miniature blank screens: one pink on the left, the other baby blue on the right. I was stupefied and immensely intrigued. I moved one hand slowly forward passing right through the floating holographic images. I gasped. The vision began to fade until not a trace remained.

I leapt off the bed, ran to the library and started documenting every aspect of this experience—one that seemed as if I had crossed an impenetrable veil. Once I released my pen, it dawned on me. I just had my first lucid dream.

CHAPTER FOURTEEN

I passed through an open private gate and parked in front of Jo's exquisite house tucked into a residential hillside in Sherman Oaks. Emerald ivy with bright red bougainvillea wove their way across walls, up to the roofline and flared out. Several trees spread their canopy over the backyard that gave shade to her regal home. After a few knocks I could hear her dogs barking.

She swung open the door. "Hi!" came her warm and welcoming voice.

On one side of her stood a muscular 90-pound Rhodesian Ridgeback named Kiba. On the other side stood Anna, a sleek 70-pound Doberman. They stood like lionesses beside her, but happily wagging their tails. Light illuminated her white skirt.

"Wow! You look beautiful," I said.

"Thank you."

"For a minute there I thought you were an angel."

I made instant friends with Anna and Kiba and then escorted Jo to my car and we headed off.

"Is it cranberry?" she asked.

I had to think a minute. "Are you trying to guess my favorite fruit juice?"

"No, the color of your car!"

"Oh!" We laughed. "Yes, cranberry."

"I love cranberry. I should think with a Jaguar as nice as this it could get you anywhere on time! Are you always late?" she jibed.

"I was born late."

"Your mother's fault or your choice?"

She seemed one beat ahead of me. "With a psychologist on our official first date I'm hardly going to talk about my mother!" I jested.

"Good point."

"You know me well enough now to know I'm a control freak with a challenged sense of timing."

"Sounds dangerous, but you're forgiven."

"For picking you up late or being born late?"

"How about I forgive you for both?"

"I knew I loved you!"

I sniffed the air trying to figure out her subtle perfume. Knowing I'd never get it, she whispered, "Eau de Roche."

"Ohhh I love the smell of gunpowder!"

We pulled in front of Chez Marc's Bistro for valet service, entered the restaurant and were shown to our table. That little Santa Monica off-beat eatery was a local secret. The evening was graced by candlelight and conversation that flowed past hors d'oeuvres, salad and into our main course. Our obsequious server, Francois, refilled Jo's wine glass; I sipped bottled water from an oversized goblet.

Jo gently took hold of my wrist, turning it to see my watch. "So, how are we doing?"

"Fine. Considering easy traffic by the time we leave. It's a two-hour drive to get to Adele's," I said, observing her smooth fingers sliding down my left hand. Physical contact felt good. It was amazing how such a seemingly inconsequential touch could send a shiver down my spine. I wanted more. I slid my right hand over and clasped my fingers around hers. "Thumb war?"

"You got it! One-two—"

As she counted, I joined in the count until we hit five and began thumb wrestling. In a matter of a couple minutes in between hysterically laughing, she pinned my thumb.

"You're in amazing shape young lady!"

"If you're going to wrestle with me, sir, better load up on protein and get a gym membership!"

All our prior telephone conversations had set the stage for our progressively accelerated connection. We discussed how Annie had become the pivotal shift for me onto this deeper search for meaning in life after finding her drunk in bed with a physician employed at the same hospital as me. It all ended in such a nightmare.

Jo was delicately bringing me out of my shell. I was learning to trust again. She too knew the challenges inherent in alcoholism, not just as a therapist in clinical practice treating patients, but from her own failed relationship with an alcoholic man with whom she was willing to spend her life. The more we talked the more we found in common. We were even able to joke around with each other on sensitive topics.

"You know," I said, "if you and I get too close, I might just end up needing therapy!"

"Now that's healthy! Get beat-up by a woman and become a monk. You shouldn't be so resistant," she responded with a broad smile.

"Hey, resistance in electricity causes current to transform into heat!" The conversation quickly moved to love. "I'm still trying to define what that is. Is love an illusion? Do we turn to others in hopes of filling a gap in our own deficiencies and feelings of emptiness?"

"No!" she insisted.

"You don't think it's all just in the head?"

"No, it isn't! It's in the heart. I know what love is. I've been in love. Many times with many things. Many people. Many creatures. Many places. I enjoy my work, but that's not my passion."

"Hey! You sound very loose!" I said jokingly.

"I didn't say *made* love! I said *in* love!"

"How'd you get so enlightened?"

She puckered her beautiful thin lips and took another sip of wine. She held the wine glass in one hand and my hand in her other. With a tender heart she looked into my eyes. "I've learned to feel," she said with just a bit of tipsiness in her voice, swirling wine around the large crystal goblet and peering through it searching for my eyes. The legs of the chardonnay crawled down the domed sides and grew clear. I could see her eyes through the glass. They glistened.

"I think my mistake has been confusing sex with love," I said.

"That's a common mistake."

"Is that a statement or my diagnosis?"

We both laughed.

"Finally, I'm prying you open!" she said.

"Frankly, I've been trying to reconstruct my whole notion of love," I said reflectively. "It's been a while since I've felt the kind of connection I feel for you, Jo." We looked straight into each other's eyes. "Opening my heart again since my break-up last year is a challenge."

"You're doing it though."

"But I'm vulnerable."

"Time heals, Richard. And sometimes with the heart you have to take risks when it feels right."

"True."

"But it is good you can talk about it."

"It's good *we* can talk about it," I said. She squeezed an ever-so-gentle but firm hold around my fingers. "Thanks for giving me the space."

Silence prevailed between us as her eyes expressed a warmth and presence as deep as our mutually growing fondness for one another. I was indeed beginning to feel again, in ways that neither of us were quite ready to put into words.

After a pleasant dinner and further warm exchanges, we began our drive south on the San Diego Freeway. We were fully content to be in one another's company with minimal conversation. However, the silence was broken when Jo was startled by a voice she heard. It wasn't my voice. "Richard! Look up!" she hollered, observing a moving prismatic light in the dusky sky heading north right above the freeway.

"I see it!"

In seconds it would be passing overhead. I immediately flashed my bright lights on and off twice, then three times in rapid succession as the gap between us was closing.

Jo nervously laughed. "They'll never see your headlights!" Immediately, the vessel's bright light went off and on twice. She looked at me, confounded.

"How'd you do that?"

I was equally amazed. "I have no idea!"

The unidentified vessel continued high above the car and presumably off in the opposite direction.

Perplexed, I asked, "How did you happen to see that?"

"Richard! My eyes were on you when I heard a voice say look up!"

CHAPTER FIFTEEN

Jo and I arrived at Adele's charming yellow house with a small unpretentious front lawn squared in by a freshly painted white picket fence. I went around to open Jo's door as she reached into the backseat and grabbed a colorful flower arrangement from a small bucket on the floor. We walked arm in arm to the house.

When Adele Tinning opened the door, Jo handed her the bouquet. "Oh! These are gorgeous! You didn't have to bring a thing. It's so nice that you would both come all the way down here to see me. Come in! Come in, please!"

The house was filled with a buzz of people chatting. Adele directed us past other people who were mingling and walking around.

"Oh! So many people here all the time!" Adele said when we reached the kitchen. "I never know who's coming or going." She laughed at herself. "Please sit down."

We took a seat at the kitchen table—the white one Adele used for her demonstrations at the Scottish Rite Temple. After fiddling with what looked like a letter, Adele slowly eased her large frame down onto the wooden chair facing us. She turned her attention to me. "When we spoke on the telephone you said you wanted me to show you this."

"Is this the reply from NASA?"

"Yes."

I turned to Jo. "Back on January 27, 1967 a fiery explosion of Apollo 1 destroyed it on the launch pad at Cape Kennedy. Astronauts Virgil Grissom, Roger Chaffee and Ed White were tragically killed."

"I remember that."

Adele picked up the story. "Astronaut Ed White had come through the table in spontaneous tapping. What was so strange was that I did not know who he was at the time so the table tapped out *astronaut*. He then tapped out a message for me to give to NASA."

"What message?"

"Two times straight now time to R.U.Y.Z." she said.

"What does that mean?"

"I didn't know at the time so I asked my husband if I should send that message to NASA. He said absolutely not!"

I recalled what Adele had told me in my phone call to her. "So she sent it!"

We all laughed. Adele then slid the letter to us that was the government's reply from a representative by the name of Harris at Cape Kennedy who was assuring her the information would be forwarded on to the 204 Board.

"Did they ever follow up with you?" Jo enquired.

"No, this letter was the last I heard from them until seven years later when two NASA scientists visited me without identifying themselves. They sat at this very table when to their amazement Ed White once again came through. The scientists finally revealed who they were and why they were here. They told me that R.U.Y.Z. stood for *rotation universal yaw zone*."

"So, what exactly does that mean?" I asked.

"It was the origin for the explosion caused by a short in the wiring."

"That's remarkable, Adele," Jo said.

"Oh! One more thing we talked about by phone," Adele said. "Here's Dr. Puharich's telephone number. He's a physician and scientist. I think you two should meet after hearing about how much you both have in common."

"Oh Adele, that's very thoughtful. Thank you. I will call him."

"You have such a lovely home," Jo said.

"Thank you, dear. It's overflowing today. There's a couple here from Illinois and another one coming from Texas. They come from all over. Isn't it wonderful?"

"They certainly love you, Adele," Jo said.

"They love God, honey. Would you both like some candy? There's some delicious sour balls I can—"

"Oh Adele, no thank you," I said, holding up my hand and gazing into her radiant blue eyes. She had such a glowing spirit about her.

"How about chocolate covered—"

"Really, we're fine, Adele," Jo politely responded.

"I even have frozen waffles in the fridge if you haven't had a chance—"

"Prefer mine toasted!" I spontaneously blurted out.

"Silly boy!" Adele snapped back without missing a beat. She looked deeply into my eyes. "Shall we start with you, dear?"

"Oh! How about we start with Jo," I suggested with a quiver. "Ladies before—"

"Richard!" Jo retorted with a smile. "You know you haven't got a shred of chivalry in your entire body!"

"Do you two know each other?" Adele jibed with a giggle. Our quick laughter shifted Adele's attention to Jo. "Okay honey, let's start with you. Both of you put your hands on the table palms down." Adele closed her eyes and pushed back her shirt sleeves above her elbows. "Now Zoro—come in dear."

"You go into a trance for this?" I inquired.

Adele opened one eye that locked like a laser beam on me. Her loving smile went right to my heart again. "Trance honey? I've been in a trance for seventy-five years," she said with an endearing smirk. Her focus turned back to Jo. "Now honey, take in a few deep breaths. You too, dear," she said to me. "Both of you now. Nice and deep, then let it out."

"Honey. Think of somebody from the other side now while our good friend here monitors." She winked at me.

Jo followed Adele's direction. Without hesitation she knew exactly who she wanted with her at the table. "Okay."

Adele looked at Jo. "Now silently in your mind ask to confirm this spirit is the one you intend to bring to the table."

Eyes still closed Jo more deeply envisioned this person. She had waited a long time for this opportunity. She also knew Adele's ability and trusted in her connection with the other side. Jo's mind was filled with a portrait of the man who had given her hope in a confusing world, the one who had taught her acceptance of disadvantaged people and the need to give everyone opportunity. He was the man who encouraged her to leave home at eighteen, at a personal loss to himself because he loved her so much, but he knew she had to escape the wrath of her malevolent mother. He was the most loving man she'd ever known and passed away far too soon. Jo's thoughts were awash with this person now long passed over. Before she even had a chance to tell us who she was bringing in, the table swiftly rose with one long edge of the table gently against her. She could feel the hair on her arms respond and chills shoot through her. The table edge kept bumping gently against her. I wasn't sure what this action indicated.

Adele at first seemed surprised, then smiled. "Oh my, this has happened so fast. I can feel this spirit here at the table. Such a very kind and loving person."

This remarkable woman had true compassion for all her guests who came to the table. She knew how difficult this was for many. Having witnessed her interactions at the Scottish Rite Temple, it was apparent that she was in every sense living simultaneously in two entirely different worlds.

Suddenly, a gust of wind sent chimes hanging just outside the open kitchen window into a wonderful musical flurry singing their harmonics on the very first breeze of the evening. Jo opened her eyes, seemingly quite stirred by the wind chimes. She looked at our sage, fully enraptured by the moment. "Oh Adele!"

The table continued bumping Jo. She began crying.

"Dear, whoever this spirit is, there's profound love at this table for you! These are hugs."

I didn't know what to make of this because no communication had begun—or so I thought. My fingers locked with Jo's. Adele glided one hand to Jo's hand and patted it gently. "Look here. For heaven's sake. You know they're not dead over there. Nothing's ever dead. Nothing in the universe ever really dies. It just gets recycled. We're all reincarnated until we reach our level of spiritual understanding that no longer requires being here. Our loved ones have the ability to be with us anytime we think of them. They're that close all the time.

They know what you're doing. They know what you're thinking. Just like us they're learning."

I could feel Jo's emotion. Adele pressed on.

"Okay now, let's have you ask confirmation that this is the spirit you want to bring in. Ask this wonderful spirit one very specific question that can be answered in three letters or three numbers."

Collecting herself, Jo quickly nodded in acknowledgement that she had completed Adele's request. "I'm asking for confirmation by giving me three letters," Jo said.

The table began tipping up and down off two legs gently producing soft clacking on the floor until all three letters were confirmed. I was doing the tabulating.

"Okay, it's D-G-S. Right?" I queried. Knowing her father's first and last name, I assumed it was him. "It's your dad!"

The wind chimes sounded again on a breeze that came through the kitchen window and sent the partially closed sheer polyester curtains dancing. Jo's throat was tight. She was nearly speechless, nodding in acknowledgment of the first three letters being correct. Tears streamed across her flushed cheeks. Through the gentle tones of the chimes settling down, Jo could truly feel her father's presence.

"Daddy loved wind chimes."

I passed more tissues to her.

"Oh, he's such a gentle soul," Adele reaffirmed.

"That perfectly describes him, Adele," Jo said.

I shook my head in amazement.

"You know, they want to connect with us as much as we want to connect with them," Adele said. A couple more questions were answered accurately. Then, Adele confessed we were running out of time. "Do you want to ask one last personal question only you and your father both know the answer to?"

We all placed our palms down on the table. Jo was pensive. She formulated her silent question, then the table tipped into me and remained against me. It caught us all by surprise.

"Ohhh!" I shouted with a startle looking over my left shoulder.

The table dropped back down flat on the floor with a thud.

"Oh my!" Adele said seriously. "What's going on?" She turned to me. "What's happening, dear?"

I wasn't sure how to quite put this into words. "I don't know! I think something just pressed down on my shoulder!" I explained, resting my right palm across my left shoulder.

Another tear fell from Jo. "I asked daddy if Richard is the one."

"Oh, now look at that! And your father confirmed it by touching him."

I was awestruck and bewildered. I looked at Jo. "Okay! That's it! I know who you were in your last life! Houdini!"

"God works in mysterious ways, doesn't He?" Adele posed with her infectious smile.

I was still massaging my shoulder. "This is pretty wild."

"But wonderful," Jo added. "Wouldn't you agree?"

"We're almost out of time, kids. I must get to my other guests soon. You can always come back you know." She turned to me. "Let's at least get your master teacher. Okay, put your hands back on the table."

Within seconds the table tipped over on two legs into my abdomen with the opposite two legs stationary on the floor. I let out a nervous laugh. Although I was trying to appear relaxed, Adele through glazed eyes picked right up on my slight incertitude.

"I can do this with one finger," she said. "Go ahead. Both of you remove your hands. Watch."

The table remained tipped on its two legs against me with only Adele's one index finger on it. Slowly, the table glided back down toward the floor. The two legs finally came to rest only inches off the ground and remained there. I was genuinely impressed because the table should have been forced to the floor by its sheer weight and gravity against only a single index finger securing it. I didn't believe I could have done what I saw her do. I was shaking my head. Adele giggled like a schoolgirl. She obviously knew something I didn't.

"Spirit works its mystery in such wonderful ways," she said.

The table at last sat on all four legs. Jo had heartfelt appreciation for my propensity toward scrutiny and caution. She had respect for that line of thinking, especially recognizing her own inclination toward sometimes being gullible and so trusting. I thought she felt protected, even comforted by my discernment.

The table tipped up, over slightly and back down several times. Adele partially opened her glazed eyes.

"Who's here, Adele?" Jo asked.

"It's my master teacher Zoro."

My eyes went wide. I remember her mentioning him at the Scottish Rite Temple. I wasn't sure what to make of that. I was thinking of the swashbuckling black-masked fictional hero Zorro on his jet-black horse and a silver sword in his scabbard out to save the day for someone. I was intrigued. "Exactly who is Zoro may I ask?"

"Zoroaster was the founder of Zoroastrianism. He was the first prophet to bring religion to our world. It's the Greek form of the old Iranian Zarathustra Spitama who was a prophet appearing hundreds of years before Jesus."

The table took what appeared to be two steps sideways. "Seems the table has a mind of its own," I suggested with surprise.

"You know, the table's like we are. It's just matter. Our spirit can travel through anything. Okay Zoro, I have two friends here with me and we want to find out this young man's master teacher—" The table walked further out of alignment and stopped about two feet askew. "Now dear, don't you give him a hard time! You behave! Straighten yourself out please." The table walked itself back in line on two legs like some kind of conscious organism. I didn't know what to make of it. I glanced over at Jo. She was enjoying it with a smile.

Adele locked one eye again on me. "Amazing isn't it?" she asked. "Now then, dear, ask Zoro who your master teacher is."

"Can you tell me—"

"In your mind, honey, not out loud. It's important we ask the right questions in order to get the right answers."

"Yes, I…I try to do that in my research."

"Now you must do it as a seeker, honey."

That truth certainly resonated. I wondered what more might Adele know about me that she wasn't saying? "This is all so new to me. I just never personally experienced anything quite like this."

Jo couldn't help herself. "Oh! A new investigation for a scientist? Now this should be your dream come true."

The table shimmered. "Zoro is laughing. He thinks you're very funny. Now remember, three tips mean yes. One tip is no. Two is partly right or doubtful."

Our banter and giggles in this very private special moment seemed to lock the three of us together. Adele closed her eyes. "Okay, ask the question again. In your mind, not out loud. Ask him to tell you the name of your master teacher, honey."

In seconds the table began to tip up and down on two legs, but the two legs never came all the way down to the floor, remaining an inch or two off the ground. It seemed once again to be defying the laws of gravity.

Jo began the alphabetical count for me, "A, B, C, D—"

"You see how the two legs never quite touch the floor? Only one spirit can do this," Adele explained.

The two legs of the table again came to rest just off the floor after the 10th downward swing representing the 10th letter of the alphabet—J. The table tipped up and down and letter by letter revealed the name of my master teacher. Before the count of the final letter, Adele opened her eyes. They were still glazed.

Jo verbalized the final letter of the word being tapped out. With uncertainty in my voice, I spoke the name with surprise. "Jesus?"

"Why yes! Jesus!" Adele said. "Oh, look at what you just discovered!" She changed her tone, raised her head eye-level with mine sensing something stirring inside me. "Are you a little nervous about that?"

"Actually, not at all. I welcome that news. I've always regarded the teachings of Jesus as sacred lessons. It's just that I was born and raised Jewish."

"Oh, that's wonderful! Did you know Jesus was Jewish?"

I dropped my chin to my chest, raised my eyes and looked dubiously at this prodigious mystic. "Adele!"

With a smile she said, "Jesus is in real strong now." The table shimmered with a steady vibration, then tipped over on two legs and pressed gently into my chest. "See how gentle Jesus is? I talk with Jesus and many of the great avatars. If only we could learn to love ourselves the way they love us." The table gently nudged me. "He's hugging you, honey. He loves you."

"I love Jesus too, Adele. "His teachings were what led me to Christianity."

"How lovely!"

"Then onto practicing Buddhism for a while."

Adele didn't flinch.

"And a little Hinduism," Jo interposed.

The table dropped to the floor.

"Oh my! How ever did you find time to sleep?" Adele exclaimed with a funny glare.

"Weekends," I said.

Jo chuckled. "He's quite the eclectic reader."

"Truth is I'm not sure if I have religion, Adele. Let me ask, are you presently a member of a church?"

"Heavens no, honey. Joining is separating. Okay kids, I must tend to other guests now."

Jo wallowed in the moment with a broad loving smile as I stood up. "Adele, we're so grateful to you for allowing us to have this session," she said.

"Oh honey, I'm grateful to you for visiting. You know, you can learn to do this same thing."

When I turned around to the wall that was directly behind me, I froze. Eye level hanging literally inches from my face was the hanger-like wire I'd seen in holographic form in my vision only days earlier when I had come out of my lucid dream. The same black rusted wire had the loop on one end and the square metallic dangling things on the other. I was stunned. And it was in the precise position in front of my face as I'd seen in the vision. Trying to catch my breath, it was all I could do to speak. I scanned and visually inspected the item on the wall, gasping and groping for something to say.

"Oh! Adele! What is this thing?"

Jo and Adele looked up from the table with no idea to what I was referring.

"What thing?" Jo asked.

"I saw this in a—" I stopped, unwilling to reveal a thing about any vision I had. "I've seen this before."

"It's a divining rod, honey," Adele explained.

"What do you do with it, Adele?"

"You douse for minerals or water, but that one's too old and wouldn't work anymore."

"I've heard of people using a divining rod. What's the origin of the name?"

"It means work that's done through God, honey."

Work that's done through God, I repeated over and over in my head. *Work that's done through God.* I was instantly struck by the fact that my lucid dream and vision were now inextricably linked to Adele. With profound awareness it seemed that the rising audiometric curve on that chalkboard might have been a gift for a new direction on one of my studies; that is, trying to understand diseases related to audiometric configurations. Might the divining rod have merely been symbolic for <u>work</u> <u>that's</u> <u>done</u> <u>through</u> <u>God</u> as it pertained to taking a thought from a dream state and materializing it into the world? I believed so. It begs the question of how much of what benefits our world originates from a Higher Threshold in a quasi-dream state. Higher forces seemed to clearly be at work interacting with me, directing and redirecting, nudging me, even intervening. It didn't escape me that the same influences appeared to be moving others around me. I reflected on Pastor Jack stepping into my life from out of the blue. Meeting Christopher and David with parallel experiences. And the sudden connections to Adele and Jo. Relationships seemed to be evolving in ways I had never seen. I couldn't imagine what was going to happen next.

Once in the car and on our way back to Los Angeles, Jo revealed that after her father passed, she would occasionally hear him call her name. That would initiate her talking with him, filling him in on the latest events in her life and a deep feeling of his presence. Our interchanges with Adele brought us much closer. I shared more detailed interpretations of my lucid dream.

Jo asked, "What was the relevance of two blank side-by-side computer screens?"

"Maybe because I'm supposed to figure this out myself?"

"How do you turn on blank screens?"

"I'm convinced the divining rod is related to work that's done through God. Perhaps there's another half to this equation. What if the two separate items were intended as analogies?"

"How so?"

"The useless outworn divining rod is to our archaic understanding of work that's done through God, as the blank screens are to a more advanced, futuristic, even better way to understand work that's done through God."

"Hmmm. I like that. So maybe what you need to do is figure out how to turn on the two screens to get your answer!"

We both laughed at such an absurd idea.

"How could I ever turn on screens from a vision?"

"Well, if you figure it out, I want to know! It would be amazing if this group of Off-Planet Intelligence is returning to try to advance life on this planet."

"I'm not convinced they ever left."

"If that's true, then some might be the Nephilim—hybrid sons of fallen angels who were not to have mingled with us, but tasked to manage and protect us," she suggested.

"Now you're sounding like Anoeschka! That's above my pay grade!"

"How do you think Anoeschka will interpret all of this with her conservative Christian upbringing?"

"Are you kidding? She'll love it. She forever quotes 1 John 4 admonishing me to test all spirit contacts to make sure they're from God. But then, how would we really know?"

"By feeling it. Adele always starts her sessions confirming who the spirit is," Jo said. "That's how she knows. That's her internal security. And like you've said many times, use discernment."

"True."

"Richard, I want to ask about the analogy you came up with around your vision with the divining rod. If your interpretation is that you're symbolically being shown that there's a more enlightened way to understand work that's done through God, how might Off-Planet Intelligence help us?"

"Let me ask you. How do you think they'd do it."

She thought about it. "Maybe they'd have to tell us the truth about God from their understanding?"

"I doubt it. We wouldn't believe it anyway. It'd just be more doctrine piled atop tons of current religious dogma. The masses might treat them like foreign invaders who are forcing us to merely believe something different. Right this moment we all are subject to some degree of risk to our lives by our varying beliefs about God, especially if you express yourself openly. Like Adele said, joining can be separating."

"Well, you're right about that. So how do we get past this?"

"I think it has to be a direct experience of God," I suggested.

"*Of* God? Or *about* God?"

"If it's about God, that's belief and dogma. If it's of God, it's a direct experience."

"Richard, I believe in God, but I think the mind of God is just too far above anyone's ability to have a direct experience. Maybe the most we can hope for is to *feel* God."

"Okay, then let's use your interpretation. If you can feel God, isn't that essentially *experiencing* Him? In our microcosmically small human capacity to understand, wouldn't that be *knowing* a part of Him?"

Jo pondered her own notion. "I see that."

"You felt your dad at the table. He hugged you. The wind came. His chimes sang beautiful music to us."

She grew a bit teary-eyed. "Yes."

"He touched your heart. He even touched me."

"Yes."

"Was that God's work?"

She was silent while composing herself. "You know, I hadn't thought about it like that," she said softly. "Yes, I think God did have His hand in it."

"Work that's done through God," I whispered.

"Yes," she said, pausing contemplatively in her velvety way. "I think that's exactly how Adele does her work."

"I think so too. So you're right. We can feel the presence of God." There was a long silence of calm between us as we sailed along the freeway on this beautiful late evening. "You know, whatever spiritual path it is that fearlessly brings us to God and maybe even unites the world, <u>not</u> <u>by</u> <u>killing</u> <u>for</u> <u>it</u>, but by our desperate soulful search to discover it, that seems to be the journey that awaits all feet that walk. I'd give up everything to know God."

CHAPTER SIXTEEN

By the time I drove Jo back to her place following time spent with Adele, we both were tired, but sleepy-eyed me was especially exhausted. The evening was an emotional peak I was still processing.

Jo unlocked her front door and I swung it open. She shooed away several moths and flying insects while I wedged one foot in the doorway.

"Out!" she hollered.

I shrugged my shoulders and in playful body language elicited wonder to what provoked her reaction.

"Not you!" she said, grabbing my arm and snapping me quickly through the doorway while still flailing her other arm at the insects. Her hard push at the door closed it. She leaned her back against the door and released a big sigh. "Would you like to come in?"

Standing in the foyer in front of her, I smiled and whispered, "I think I am."

"I mean come in for a cup of coffee or something!"

"No thanks. I don't do stimulants and I want to sleep tonight. Caffeine would keep me up."

"Oh, I forgot!"

"I only have a short drive back to the house anyway. I'll be fine."

I took hold of the back of Jo's synthetic white fox coat to help her off with it. I noticed how she swung her head more than casually close to mine and her face slowly passed by my lips. Weaving pheromones seemed to overpower the scent of any perfume in the air. She slowly pulled one arm up from the narrow shaft of her coat and looked upward into my curly beard. "You're zonked too?"

I felt more overcome by my affection for her than the fatigue. Her beautiful presence came even nearer. My complexion must have turned ruddy. She removed her arm from the other sleeve. I wanted her, but I also knew I better get out of there. Was this to be the ultimate test of celibacy, or I wondered, was she flirting with danger because she knew she was safe? It was alchemical attraction for us both. All the senses but common sense was working. We had never even kissed. We looked into each other's eyes. I was melting. My imagination wasn't helping matters either. I had to get a grip. Why was I provoking, even torturing myself?

As we stood face to face, I'm sure she was anticipating a goodnight kiss. "I'd be interested in hearing sometime how long you think you might be on your quest."

She leaned in and swung her arms around me. I was in trouble. I put my arms around her and brought her into my chest in an embrace. I was so torn. It was intoxicating. She drove her fingers through my beard and pulled my face close. Our lips almost touched as we breathed the same air. I was drunk with affection.

I pulled back. I held her shoulders with both hands and looked deeply into her gorgeous eyes. "Celibacy's been good for me," I whispered. "It's taken such a long time for me to finally feel directed and focused. I know I'm guided and watched. Something's embedded in my life in ways I don't yet understand. I don't even have the words. I've got to stay true to this journey, Jo, and do my best to figure things out and change the things I can change. The old Richard has to die."

"I love the old Richard!" she said.

We stood there eye to eye. I was overjoyed with her in my life. Everything was so comfortable. So easy. So natural. "I have the deepest feelings for you, Jo, but my heart is opening faster than I can manage. I can't juggle this quest at the same time enduring this uncontrollable, overpowering attraction I have for you. I'm an inch away from letting go of this entire search so I can give you all of me, but I can't let it go. I just can't."

"Richard, I respect that. I don't want to be a distraction. I think time will take things along a course that will be comfortable for us both."

"That means a lot to me, Jo."

I drew her to me in a long and loving embrace, then fondly looked again into her eyes. "You're so beautiful. In so many ways. Now, if I don't get on the road this minute, I'm going to have to bunk down in your spare bedroom."

She laughed. "That wouldn't be so bad."

Laughing at myself I opened the door which brought in a large moth that landed directly on her shoulder. She jumped up and down then swooshed the air near it trying to flick it off—shrieking all the while—but purposely kept missing it because she didn't want to hurt it. I quickly closed the door.

"Ohhh! Get it off! Get it off!" she moaned as though it was some awful gargoyle.

"Relax," I said, laughing as I extended my open hand to the moth. "It's just another creature looking for the light."

I snatched it off her shoulder in a single sweep of my hand, gently sealed my fingers around it, kissed Jo on the cheek and left with the moth.

CHAPTER SEVENTEEN

Sailing along the freeway heading back home after my treasured connection with Jo, my elation from our time together culminated in my memory of what her dad had expressed about me. I was certain she too was the one and like she said, we'd figure it out in time.

As I continued driving, I reflected on my session with Adele. If spirit which defines our presence manifests in a cycle of what we understand to be life and death, this cycle seemed to reasonably explain what I had been feeling for so long. That void. A yearning to fill the void. A knowing without explanation that there is so much more that we do not understand about ourselves and Spirit. For me it was a longing and hunger for reconnection.

A horn blast came out of nowhere and instantly rattled me back into the car. I abruptly turned the wheel enough to get back into my own lane and realized I had just fallen into a stupor with all my introspection. I brought my excessive speed back down to 65 mph and set the cruise control. I only caught a few hours' sleep the night before working way too late into the early morning. I realized I was in a bit of a fog.

I lowered the window. The whirling wind sent my full head of hair into a tizzy, but in seconds it was lulling me further toward sleep. I closed one eye for a moment, then the other hoping it would give me some reprieve. It didn't. I closed the window. The clock showed 1:10 a.m. Twenty more minutes and I knew I'd be snuggled into my warm bed. However, I was battling potentially deadly fatigue. I considered pulling over and sleeping off the drowsiness, but I was certain I could work through it. Twenty minutes was nothing.

I took in a deep breath, blew it out and clicked on the radio. Led Zeppelin was screaming Stairway to Heaven. I joined in exercising my vocal cords, but the fatigue came at me in another wave. My eyelids were heavy and the music only drove my focus further from the freeway. I turned off the radio and opened the window again, trying to fight sleep with swords of consciousness. The clock hadn't moved—still twenty minutes to go. Unbelievable! I bumped up the cruise control to seventy-five, ten miles over the limit. I didn't care. I'd be back to my house that much sooner.

But even with such optimism, seconds were becoming formidable. I felt my body slipping away. Rays of darkness pierced my vision and an unexpected larger wave overcame me. In the next moment a meditative calm entered me. The tire-road noises disappeared. Wherever I was I'm sure I thought it was safe and comfortable as relaxation moved in. In the distance I heard what sounded like a holy cherubim choir quickly coming upon me until I was immersed in its gorgeous, melodic harmonies. Then, with no warning at all, it came at me with horrific deafening assault. It was ear-shattering and frightening. It scared the living hell out of me.

My eyes snapped open and I realized I must have almost fallen asleep. The mellifluous choir dissolved into the roar of tire-road noises. The speedometer was still holding at 75, but the car was frightfully too close to the right edge of the freeway and fortunately, no vehicle had been in front of me. The clock showed 1:11 a.m., only another minute had elapsed. It seemed like forever to me.

I bumped the cruise control up to 80. Memory of the sound of the choir played over and over in my mind. It had been enchanting and magical—angels actually singing to me. Wild. The sound was that of a sacred choir, but scary in the way it had come at me so unexpectedly and so powerfully. Regardless, I knew that it may have just prevented a crash.

I focused on the hilly horizon, figuring that if I kept my eyes off the repetitious markers and dividing lines, my mind would not wander. But my body was heavy again. My light oxford loafers felt like lead on my feet. I was going to lose it again and this time I knew I might not be so lucky. I saw a sign for the next exit only one mile ahead. Stimulants or not I knew that was my cue for a cup of coffee. I had no choice. I had to get off the highway.

But before I knew it my mind was adrift again. The monotony of the tires jolting over every twelve-foot section of the pavement slowly faded away. Quietude again came upon me like a friend. My eyes no longer saw the road. They were in that fog and mist between drowsiness and sleep. In the distance I heard the most enchanting, mesmerizing choir singing to me. In rapid voluminous progression it sang louder and louder until it came at me again with explosive assault screaming for my very life.

This time my eyes popped open catching rows of high lampposts shooting past me, brightness from the dark. The Jag had drifted into another lane on the left and was about to crash head-on into the rear of a huge tandem trailer. My instinct was to slam on the brakes which locked. The needle of the speedometer dropped to zero. I pushed back into my seat prepared for impact. The car fishtailed with a thud, but I was still flying forward. The rubber tires smoked and scorched along the pavement. I imagined the crash, seconds away, into or under the rear of the enormous truck. It seemed inevitable. Unavoidable.

In a flash I reacted. I let off the brake to regain control and threw the steering wheel hard left. There was no time to think—just do. The front end veered left going into another left lane and a narrow-paved emergency median strip. The rear end followed, but overcompensation and momentum kept the car sideways clicking over reflector bumps like machine gun fire. I felt swallowed up by the sound of the truck's airhorn as my sedan advanced alongside the tandem trailer nearly kissing the entire length of it. I sailed past it. The smoke, smell and sound of burning rubber was everywhere, but even louder were the screams of the spectacular choir quickly fading into memory.

The car was suddenly lost in a flurry of dust and dirt. Gravel thrashed the underbelly. The huge trailer sped by with its airhorn still blaring. Although I couldn't see a thing through the thick night air and dust, I knew a concrete bridge abutment was somewhere ahead. In my mind, I was already hearing the sound of exploding glass and crushing metal.

All this took place in a matter of only a few seconds. The Jag came to rest in a cloud along the median facing oncoming traffic with the passenger door only inches from a chain-link fence dividing the highway. It was over. The car was intact and so was I. Memory of the choir played over and over. My mind was reeling in a hunting-gathering mindset of understanding. I was thinking, probing, searching. I was certain a terrible crash or even my life had just been saved by remarkable spiritual intervention. I had never heard such choral singing like that anywhere, coming out of nowhere, and so timely.

Once the air started clearing, the rearview mirror captured the massive concrete bridge abutment maybe fifteen feet away. I was shaking. The more I thought about it the more I realized that marathon could have cost my life if not for the choir. I sat in the darkness and listened for the cherubim choir, but all that was present was the rapid thumping of my heartbeat and the whoosh of cars swallowed up in the late-night mist.

A single thought crystallized. I once again recalled Adele's wisdom. Each of us has a guardian angel, a guide from the other side who protects and guides us. Our challenge is to listen. And I was beginning to listen more attentively. I offered my deepest gratitude to the angels of the choir who saved the night.

CHAPTER EIGHTEEN

One look in the mirror and I knew I had to do something about it. My hair was getting the wild look of my buddy Sid. I called Angie at the salon who was able to squeeze me in at noon. Once in the chair she started cutting, pulling, trimming, and running her fingers through my hair and neck. I closed my eyes in the pure sensate pleasure of it. Her soothing, almost hypnotic tugs pushed me deeply into relaxation. I became oblivious to the din of chatter around me. That was exactly the state of mind where I liked to bring a challenge, the quiet space of the mind where I would work to resolve an issue.

On that day, the Palm Springs encounter only a couple weeks away was occupying my thoughts. The invitation was mind-bending to say the least. Beyond that, I couldn't get a handle on what might unfold during the event itself. That left me with two powerful considerations. Had I been asked to come alone because they were going to share knowledge or technology with me that might help the planet, and such contact would have to remain private? Or was this going to be an abduction? That is, come alone so no one will witness the abduction. I was torn and I was feeling the pressure.

Angie continued to cut and trim while chatting with her co-worker Ridonna who was cutting another client's hair in the adjacent chair. They giggled and laughed, but I was somewhere else. I was seeking the inner sanctum of peace, stillness and quiet. It is much like doing a back float in the open ocean where you soon become unaware of the water. I slipped ever-so-much deeper into relaxation with the mind quickly quieting. My breathing was slow. I had found silence between the thoughts. I was in the deepest meditative state.

When Angie finished, she slapped her hand down so hard on my shoulder that it ejected me right out of the moment. My eyes snapped open with a startle and they fixed on my reflection in the large mirrored wall. Frozen in my seat looking straight into the mirror I saw the hazel of my own eyes staring back. They had more clarity and focus than I'd ever seen in my life.

"You're gonna get whistles from them babes now, Doc!" Angie submitted. "What do you think?"

I was in shock. How was I able to see my own image in the mirror perfectly without my glasses? I caught Angie's reflection. She was bathed in golden light. How was such an extraordinary thing possible?

I quickly turned my head away from the mirror and looked directly at Angie beside me. This was confirmation. She was standing right there with golden light all around her. Her black skin was radiant, sparkling with sheen as though sprinkled with fairy dust. Her eyes were scintillating.

"Well? What do you think, Doc?" Angie asked again.

I looked back in the mirror at Angie and me. We were both bathed in this golden light. I could see my shocked facial expression. I turned and stared at her beside me. The glow persisted. It was really difficult to understand what was happening. I must have unconsciously released a long baffling groan.

Angie was taken aback. Her smile turned to disappointment. "You don't like it, honey?"

I turned my head and opened my eyes wider, taking in more of the salon. In the waiting room a woman and a young child were seated. They had the identical golden glow all around them. A man seated alone had the golden glow. Everything had that commanding golden presence. It was almost as if the room had become crystallized, alive with sparkling light in a captivating display of refractions, emanations, light peaks, rays and spires. I felt like I had just stepped into some kind of sacred space. I was seeing with new eyes and new vision.

"Well, come on!" Angie pleaded, waiting and frustrated.

Dazed by this phenomenal new vision, I was dumbfounded. When I tried to think logically, it seemed absurd that I was seeing all of this perfectly without my glasses. This I knew was impossible. In this precious moment I had forgotten that *all things are possible!* My old patten emerged with the old memory that I was blind as a bat without glasses. Acting out of pure impulse and habit, failing to recognize this monumental miracle, I said, "Angie, I can't see without my glasses!" These flippant words slipped off my lips like white water rapids down a river—no second thought of the untruth I had spoken.

But I could see. Perfectly. I could see everything except the very gift—literally—of the vision I'd been given. Angie handed me my thick glasses which didn't hold plastic lenses but actual glass to help me see better.

"So?" she begged.

Instantly upon putting on my glasses the wonder was gone, the golden lights ceased. Like a light switch instantly thrown, it all abruptly ended. Nothing remained but a look of shock, horror and confusion on my face. "Oh shit! It's gone!"

"The hair? I mean it is a haircut!" Angie said with a chuckle.

I snatched my glasses back off my face and looked around the room, but it was too late. Everything was blurred and out of focus. I looked at the little girl, but in so doing, couldn't tell if that was a girl or a boy sitting in the waiting area. It was over. I put my glasses back on and realized I couldn't even see well with them. I was beside myself. My old miserable nearsightedness had returned.

"Oh Angie!" I uttered, realizing what I'd done, realizing my err in mindfulness, recognizing how my dismissal, even disbelief in the miracle of perfect vision had cost me the very vision itself. "Ohhh!" I moaned.

Angie threw her hands up, "Come on now, I've been cutting hair for twenty-two years—"

"No, no, no—"

"Then what's going on with you, baby?"

I looked up at her, unsure of what to say. Where do you even begin? "I'm...I'm late, Angie! Just running late!" Tears filled my eyes. "It looks fine!"

I got out of the chair and moved right to the mirror to be absolutely certain one last time that the golden lights were no longer present. They weren't. They were gone.

Angie shook her head. "Maybe you're workin' too much, Doc."

Ridonna winked at me. "Maybe you need to get more sizzle from your steak, honey, if you know what I mean."

The girls giggled, but I couldn't look at either of them. I reached into my pocket and drew out some cash. I felt embarrassed, disgraced by my thoughtless action. I was defeated. I had cheated myself through my own stupidity. I put ample cash down on the counter and headed out. I didn't care how much was on the counter. It had already cost me too much.

When I reached my car on the street, I tried to compose myself before I got in. My vision rolled skyward to the puffy white clouds contrasted against the deep sapphire sky. I stood there shaking my head in dismay, then got in the car and sat motionless behind the wheel. I knew I had experienced another miracle and in its very midst threw it entirely out of consciousness. This was no less a miracle than the choir which I was coming more and more to believe hadn't just saved a crash, but my life.

Sitting quietly long enough I saw past the travail to a bigger picture. Without being able to put my finger on it, something was changing. Of course it was rather out of the ordinary to suddenly open your eyes in a hair salon and find yourself in a crystal city on this planet, something most of us don't experience in a lifetime. But it was more than that. It was beyond that. There was something inside me, deep inside which was changing. Perhaps it had to do with my changing perception of life. After all, it had not been that long ago that I considered life to be far more mundane where we all grope for Spirit. But something was different now. Had my perfect eyesight been a gift through a Heavenly Source?

More and more I was coming to recognize the presence of these miracles with a new understanding. *We must learn to accept them, embrace them, not challenge them. We must learn to give gratitude for each and every one of them.* And like the waitress with poor service at the Good Earth Restaurant, once again, forgiveness was on the table. I had to forgive myself for my blindness and mindlessness.

Sitting motionless once again in my car, I found myself this time giving gratitude to God. "Thank you. Thank you. Thank you."

CHAPTER NINETEEN

One Sunday afternoon the neighborhood kids flagged me down.

"We have a question," Johnny stated affirmatively. "How can we get to see UFOs?"

"We've never seen them except in those pictures," Logan said.

"And we want to see them close up and personal," Kevin insisted.

Little Maddie looked at me with disappointment. "Kevin's father says they're not real."

"Now hold on kids. I can't make them just appear like a magician. Most of the time during the day they look like stars so you can't just look into the sky and boop they appear. They're pretty much invisible," I explained.

"Then how do you make them uninvisible?" Kevin asked.

If my Good Earth Restaurant interchanges with the waitress and the Voice were any indicators, developing love and compassion certainly seemed key. "You know how important it is to eat right." The children were attentive. "Well, it's just as important to think right. Maybe it's time for us to stop judging each other." I reflected on Adele's wisdom. "We don't know why people do what they do or say what they say. Maybe all we need to do is forgive everybody for everything and just be kind, good people. When we can forgive and love each other, which will open the heart to other possibilities, maybe that's how we'll discover our connection to other worlds and maybe even come to know this Off-Planet Intelligence. We have to first demonstrate it among ourselves."

Johnny responded quickly. "Okay, we're going to sit on our lawn until we see them."

The children thanked me and with excitement merged onto the Anderson's front lawn. I headed into the house to prepare a salad for lunch. I was still in the kitchen when I heard hollering and thrashing at my front screen door. Johnny and Logan were feverishly banging their fists against the frame of the screen door.

"They came! They're here!" they screamed unable to contain themselves.

"Come on, Richard! Come on!" Logan shouted, peering through a rip in the screen. "Hurry! Hurry! Hurry-up!"

I did not know what to believe, but their excitement seemed to speak for itself. This caught me totally by surprise. I held back Shadow from escaping through the doorway and in the next moment I was yanked outside by the two kids. They kept tugging unremittingly on my sleeves, lurching me forward down the sidewalk. My bare feet were picking up pebbles along the way.

"Ai ai ai ai—ouch! Wait!" I mumbled, hobbling along on my tiptoes trying to avoid hazards on the path, my shirt pulled a half foot ahead of me.

The kids couldn't wait. They ran ahead, guiding me across the street as though to some mountaintop. "Hurry, Richard! You've got to see!"

"Okay, okay!"

We all joined Kevin and Maddie on the Anderson's front lawn and stared off into the relatively clear sky. With unabated excitement Kevin hollered to me, "There! Over there! There's only two now, but—"

"There!" Maddie insisted, pointing wildly.

Johnny studied the sky and tried to reestablish his gaze, pointing up at an angle. "They were right...there! There they are! I see them! There's three now!"

"There were four!" shouted Kevin.

I was as wild with anticipation as the kids. "Okay, calm down. Let's look together. I don't quite see them."

"I see four!" Maddie said.

"I see five now!" screamed Johnny.

I squatted down directly behind Johnny, looking over his shoulder in the direction to where he was pointing. Once my eyes adjusted to the brightness, I saw what appeared to be glowing white stars high above the horizon. "Wow! You're right. How about that!"

"You see?" Logan asked. "You see?"

"It's just like you told us, Richard!" Kevin said with matter-of-fact confirmation.

"You kids are amazing!"

I was flabbergasted. My eyes moved from the stars to the children, back and forth. I observed their array in the sky, just for a moment, matched the formation of the kids standing with me on the lawn. *Coincidental?* I wondered.

"Kevin!" I said firmly. "Get your dad. Right now!"

"He'll be mad!"

"No he won't! Hustle though."

A smile shot across Kevin's face. He took off running down the block toward his house a couple hundred feet away. My attention remained glued to the sparkling lights.

"Hey! They're moving again!" shouted Maddie.

My mind was reeling. Might we all have a star in the heavens? Is this our Heavenly Family? Might they even be our genetic origin? I was convinced we're more linked to these Intelligences than we presently understand.

In a matter of minutes, Larry Thomas made his way over with attitude. There was fire in his eyes. "Do I need to call the police?"

Maddie pointed to the sky as Larry towered over her. "Look, Mr. Thomas. The police won't be able to catch them."

Not amused, Larry stared at me. I smiled back, "Look, like Maddie said."

Johnny interceded. "There were five, but there's only four now."

Larry begrudgingly turned around, feeling like a sucker pulled into a back-alley scam. "Where?" he asked with meanness in his voice, his squinting eyes constantly drifting over to me standing to his right waiting for a response. "I don't see a thing!"

"You're not looking, Larry," I said with sincerity, but I could feel his hostile presence.

"I don't see anything!" he insisted.

"There!" Maddie indicated, pointing to a wide clearing near some clouds. "They're looking right at you, Mr. Thomas!"

I moved over to Larry, stood behind his left shoulder and pointed. Shading his eyes with one hand, Larry placed his fingers more tightly across his forehead and gazed intently into the brightness—searching.

I looked at him. Were we not cut from the same cloth? I knew I had been no different than Larry in my own challenges, doubts and fears, something that had become a lifelong battle to which I was still trying to master. Standing with Larry my only feelings were ones filled with compassion and understanding. I sensed this was a life-changing moment for him. Witnessing vessels like this instantaneously alters reality.

Finally, Larry saw them. There were four incredibly bright lights, far larger than any stars and not like anything he'd ever seen. But for Larry, they couldn't be stars, not during the day, even Larry knew that was impossible. He was searching for an explanation. "Those...things...they've got to be helicopters!" he rather indignantly suggested, instantly dismissing the possibility that they indeed could be something he'd never seen.

I again saw myself reflected in his rationalization. I saw the denial, the resistance, the refusal to believe something in its very presence in front of your own eyes; the unwillingness to acknowledge something different than anything ever seen before. It was the hair salon vision replaying itself, but this time with Larry. I kept wondering, *what is this human nature of ours that obstructs recognition of anything outside our belief system? How is it we can witness something phenomenal and in its very presence deny it? Is it we who stand in our own way of a new reality?*

"They've got to be helicopters," Larry reaffirmed.

"No, they aren't, Mr. Thomas," Maddie protested. "Johnny has helicopters and they don't look like that."

"Yeah! Those are UFOs, Mr. Thomas!" Logan insisted.

Larry was trapped. He didn't know what he was seeing, but one thing he did know. They weren't UFOs. For him, they didn't exist. He grunted.

Suddenly the stars rapidly changed formation and did a few loops. The kids screamed with delight and excitement at every movement.

"Man, that is so cool!" Johnny said.

Larry didn't move or utter a sound. His eyes were fixed on the sky, his mouth remained open and he could not remove his gaze from what was in the throes of altering his reality.

Johnny was elated. "Wow! Do you see that?"

"Shiiiiit!" Larry finally grumbled, his eyes still glued on the vast blue sky and amazement frozen into his expression.

Then the stars disappeared. The children's focus remained on the sky, searching through the depths of the blue hoping for another appearance.

"Where'd they go, Richard?"

"No idea, Johnny."

"Now do you believe in UFOs?" Maddie asked Larry.

"Well!" he said almost on a gasp. "Those...flying things, we don't really know what they were."

Maddie peered up trying to make eye contact with Larry. She lit up with a warm smile and an open heart. "That's why they're called UFOs, Mr. Thomas. No one knows what they are."

CHAPTER TWENTY

Although Jo and I were holding back sensate pleasures, our relationship was evolving at a rapid pace. Almost daily we were engaged in telephone conversations and were meeting over lunches or dinners. For me, the closer sense of intimacy was near, but would simply have to evolve in its own time without attempting to push the river.

Meanwhile, I made initial telephone contact with physician, scientist and inventor Andrija Puharich, MD. Our long and provocative telephone conversation peaked our mutual interests, although discussing such sensitive topics over the phone kept us both from going into much detail. He alluded to government affiliation of some kind and was vague about it being in the past or present. Despite that concern, a meeting was set up at Jo's home. I cautioned her to be diligent about revealing my own deeply personal experiences, especially about a voice I had not yet identified. Jo and I were uncertain where Dr. Puharich might stand on these matters. We certainly needed to learn first about any entanglements he might have with the government.

It was a beautiful day with sunlight illuminating the house when the three of us got together. We settled down in the living room after Jo served up iced herbal tea and some home-baked cookies.

"Richard, it's good we had a chance to get to know each other a little."

"Yes Andrija, I feel the same. I'm glad we have finally met."

Dr. Puharich was mid-sixties, affable, maybe a foot shorter than me with a white, untrimmed moustache and grey-black Einstein wild hair.

"Have you thought more about the possibility of helping to develop my patent on the bone conduction device we spoke about?" he asked.

"Actually, I've already discussed it with an industry manufacturer. They talked about putting it under review to see if it's cost effective. So, we'll have to wait."

"Okay," he said, placing the palms of his hands across his small belly bulge. "Jo, Richard tells me that you're in the throes of your PhD dissertation in psychology on alien abduction."

"Yes. I was approved to do a descriptive study on people reporting UFO abduction."

He slightly smiled. "Fascinating."

"I've already interviewed probably fifty people reporting abduction," Jo said.

"Wonderful," he replied. "That's become a popular subject matter."

I was proud of Jo's work. "If I won't embarrass her, I might mention that MIT is soon to hold a closed-to-the-press conference on alien abduction, bringing together the most prominent research scientists on the topic. They invited Jo to present her dissertation results."

"You must be pleased, Jo," he said, his blue eyes bright.

"And a little nervous!"

"What are your findings?"

"The most intriguing result so far is finding 95 percent of my subjects are reporting abduction by what we've identified as the Greys."

"I'm not surprised," he said." What about the other 5 percent?"

"Well, I don't know if it'll be statistically significant or not, but so far it comprises encounters with tall, loving, ethereal beings."

Dr. Puharich nodded. "That'll be a contribution to the literature."

"It's the first phenomenological study ever done on alien abduction," I said.

"I'd like to read it when it's done," he genuinely asked.

Jo finally spurred him to cross the confidential barrier. "Richard told me you have also had your own direct contact," she said. "Can you share what that was?"

"Are you familiar with Uri Geller?"

I immediately reacted, "The spoon bender?"

Dr. Puharich was soft-spoken with thin lips that sometimes seemed on the edge of breaking into a broad and cordial smile projecting a sense of knowing more than he was sharing. "Spoon bending was a small part of what he could do."

"Wasn't he discredited on a television show?" I queried.

"He appeared on the *Johnny Carson Show* in 1973 and was unable to properly demonstrate his true abilities. They extended far beyond what he was discredited for. He and I worked together. There's still a large group that does not like us. Uri is one of the mediums who established contact through an extraterrestrial voice that called itself Spectra. They said their species is known as Hoova."

"How far is Hoova from Earth?" Jo asked.

"They said one million five-hundred thousand light-years."

This information immediately inspired me to divulge my own experiences with the mysterious voice in the hope that Dr. Puharich would be able to shed light on its origin, but I could reveal nothing. I still sensed I couldn't until I was able to determine if he could be trusted. This I knew would take time and maybe only after building a friendship.

"How did this voice of Spectra come through?" Jo asked.

"One way was through Uri's channeling. We'd hear it appear in the room above our heads. But I've also heard it through tape recording."

I didn't understand. "What do you mean tape recording?"

"We would typically set up a standard tape recorder. Then Spectra would start the recording followed by them speaking to us somewhere in the room. And of course, our voices are recorded on tape as well as Spectra's."

"In real time?" Jo asked.

"Yes."

"So you're interacting with this group?" I inquired.

"Yes. We ask questions. Spectra answers them or Spectra talks and provides a perspective and we listen."

"If it's recorded, then I assume you must have quite a collection of tapes."

"Richard, I wish. At the end of a session after we listen to Spectra and our recorded selves, if we don't erase the tape, the tape literally vanishes."

Jo wasn't sure she heard this correctly. "Right in front of your eyes? The whole cassette disappears?"

"The whole cassette. They're capable of materializing and dematerializing physical objects in our world. We scientists don't yet understand these remarkable dynamics in the laws of physics."

"What else have you witnessed that disappeared?" Jo asked.

"Well, it's both dematerialization and reappearance or materialization of various items like jewelry, keys, metal rings, even a gun I had—"

Perplexed, I asked, "Just to be clear, this is all in your presence so you see it happen?"

"Yes...usually. However, other times things have just gone missing and reappear later."

While Jo was bright-eyed, watching and listening with hyperfocus on his every word, he seemed to want to reassure me of the veracity of his claims. "It is true," he said without blinking. "I've witnessed all these things and so much more. Again, these are experiences that are very challenging to not only convey to someone, but to accept as true when you haven't experienced them. We're talking about things most people would think were impossible."

I certainly knew that truth. "Isn't that a natural human inclination?"

"Yes. However, back then I had formed a group comprising experimental and theoretical physicists who also witnessed these remarkable events with Uri and me. I might mention that eventually Uri underwent rigorous scientific scrutiny at the Stanford Research Institute and in turn was fully authenticated with respect to his abilities."

"That's extraordinary, Andrija," Jo softly said.

I repeated Jo's approbation followed by a long pause. "Let me get back to the voice for a second. Does this voice sound human?"

"Good question, Richard. Sometimes yes. Sometimes mechanical or electronic, but that could be attributed to unknown circumstances."

"So is Spectra a living organism like us?" I asked.

"We can't be sure, but one of the contactees I have worked with describes

Spectra as a social memory complex."

"Has this species ever been to our planet?" I asked.

"They told us they land on Earth about every six thousand years."

"When were they here last?" I queried.

"Six-thousand years ago."

"So, then they're returning?" Jo posed.

"They were uncommitted about that. They said because of our tendency around fearing them as well as worshipping them—two extremes—they're hesitant. Neither trait is a good human characteristic they told us. They said the one to worship is God."

"You mean they believe in God?" I asked, startling even myself by the possibility.

"They told us we have a soul and through our souls we connect to God."

"Andrija, that's fascinating," I said, inspired by this confirmation. "If we assume what we now see in our skies is not the Hoova group, is there any other group you know of that uses a voice to speak to us?"

"Well, let me back up. I was friends with an East Indian Hindu scholar, Dr. D. G. Vinod. He was one of the most remarkable mediums I've encountered. He was the first to channel the Hoova for me. This extraterrestrial group Hoova at that time was identifying themselves as the Nine. We had several sessions on multiple occasions with others present during those channelings."

"So, Nine means exactly what?" queried Jo.

"They said nine principles or personalities comprise the Hoova group. They have no physicality although they can create a body if needed. Together they are apparently an enlightened source. I was fortunate to get a book published about these early experiences with the Nine through Dr. Vinod and Uri."

What he was sharing seemed to offer a reasonable explanation for my encounter at age nine. That Being of Light might have just materialized and dematerialized right inside my parent's home which would also explain no breach of the house. "Where can I get that book, Andrija?"

"Maybe at a used bookstore. If you locate that book you'll see quite a lot of details about my research and experiences, some mathematical formulae and so forth. Too much to get into here and frankly a lot to contemplate and digest."

Setting down my tea, I had more questions. "With respect to the Nine, did they ever appear to you in our physical world?"

"No. It was only auditory contact. As an expert in the science of hearing and the transmission of sound, Richard, this ought to be right up your alley."

"Yes definitely, the coincidence has not escaped me." Thinking and nibbling on a cookie, excited to learn what might unfold next, I was moved by the parallels in our mutual experiences. My attention was fully on Dr. Puharich. "So…this voice. With respect to both Spectra and the Nine, do you trust this voice and information revealed?"

"I hold a certain reverence for these remarkable beings. It's a deeply personal experience," he qualified. Charisma rolled off him like charm around a Hollywood star. "They *seem* benevolent and to have our best interest at heart."

"Are any UFOs associated with these experiences?" Jo asked.

"Not necessarily at the time of communication, but my group has certainly documented the presence of UFOs."

Jo gave Dr. Puharich a quizzical look. "Did you capture photographic images?"

"Yes. I have good photographic evidence. How about you, Richard?"

"No. Frankly there's so much controversy and accusations of fraud around UFO film and photo images, I never had such interest. You know, Andrija, years ago one of the most credible books on this subject matter was written by Ruth Montgomery."

"*Aliens Among Us?*"

"Yes! I was certain she was right on. Do you have an opinion on this?"

"The term aliens I think can be a misnomer. It's a little scary. Very 1950s. A better classification would be species. I suspect other species could be here."

"Could be?" Jo queried. "On what basis do you say that?"

"I was tasked to carry out…well, I was involved in a quiet project that oversaw kids with psychokinesis, extrasensory perception, telepathic communication capabilities and so forth. Really extraordinary abilities."

"Extraordinary abilities or extraterrestrial abilities?" I questioned. "That is, if other species are among us."

He kind of smiled, shrugged and didn't answer the question. I was feeling he knew more than he was willing to share, but perhaps we both were just testing each other.

Jo asked, "How did this all start for you?"

He took in a deep breath and sat taller on the sofa. He had our attention. "Long before I got my medical degree at Northwestern, I had always been interested in the paranormal. So, a government agency recognizing my interest invited me to participate in ongoing research of children with extraordinary abilities. We used a Faraday cage I had built. Once you start working around something considered outside normal parameters, it becomes quite normal. There were about a hundred progenies whose progress I followed over the years. One of them has remained close to me."

"Well, if extraterrestrials are among us, what's the purpose?" I asked.

"I suppose one purpose would be to step up our genetic code."

Jo furrowed her brow. "What does that mean?"

"I think there's enough science to know that if we're left to natural human evolution, we would eventually develop extraordinary abilities. But that would take countless millennia. Understand if extraterrestrials are among us, it would accelerate our human genetic development."

I pondered this possibility. "That's extraterrestrials interbreeding with humans?"

"Not entirely...but kind of," he said.

That was a stunner. There was dead silence.

Jo and I stared at each other. Although aghast, Jo gathered her wits. "Oh Andrija! Isn't there a moral conflict with this?"

"If it's a matter of advancing the human race, many people don't look at this as a moral issue. I say theoretically, if there happens to be a group of extraterrestrials much like ourselves, and they have superior biochemical abilities that far exceed all of Earth's planetary races, that's perceived as progress. If not for that kind of intervention and leaving the human race to its own natural evolution, the Nine tell us it could take a quarter million years to attain a higher level of development. Genetic bioengineering would be a skillful shortcut. As a medical doctor, although I'm not involved in any genetic coding, on a theoretical level it could be a long-term benefit to humanity."

"Would it ever be possible to meet one of your star children?" I asked.

His response was immediate. "Yes. I could introduce you to a young gentleman with the kind of abilities we're talking about."

"You mean right here on this planet?" Jo asked.

He giggled like a schoolboy. "Yes! Right here on terra firma Los Angeles." He looked over at me. "He's in his thirties. His name is Timothy. Want me to set it up with you?"

"Yes! Certainly!" I said.

"You can ask him questions. Put something in an envelope, seal it and he'll tell you what's in it. That kind of thing through extrasensory perception."

I was captivated, and perhaps this proposed encounter would offer some verification of what he was indicating. I liked him. I was fully drawn in. Nevertheless, he was so glib. Sharing with strangers what seemed to me to be highly classified information was concerning. I was glad I had been reserved in revealing anything about the Voice.

Over a period of hours with Dr. Puharich so engaging, our conversation evolved into more and more depth and personal information with all three of us talking about ourselves, our work, beliefs and religion until I asked a poignant, probing question. "Andrija, you said that the Nine mentioned we're a species full of fear and false idols. May I ask if you were ever fearful of the extraterrestrials?"

"I trusted the group of extraterrestrials who spoke with us. I had much less trust with the humans we worked with."

"What does that mean?" Jo asked.

"Taking what you know is true, presenting what is outside mainstream science and presenting it to mainstream scientists, the very group needed to authenticate the truth, is challenging. Attempts were made to discredit not just Uri, but me, my work, my team. It was a very tough, disheartening period."

"How did you make it through?" Jo asked.

"Look, I'm a scientist at heart with a great desire to learn and discover—like Richard here. Before that book about Uri I mentioned, an earlier one in 1959 was published, *The Sacred Mushroom*. The reason I mention it at all is after its publication it raised such hell that a wing of the government went out and tried to confiscate every copy they could get their hands on."

"Did they succeed?" I asked.

"I think they did. The final straw sometime later was an arson fire in my home in Ossining, New York, which burned to the ground along with some of my research and books."

I gasped. "What a terrible thing!"

"Yes, it was. But we all made it out alive even though I did lose irreplaceable things."

"That must have been emotionally traumatic, Andrija!" Jo said.

"It was, but the reason I mention this at all is that you asked me about fear of extraterrestrials. No, I don't fear them. I had reasons to fear humans. After the fire I fled to Mexico for my safety among friends for three years during that uncertain period until I could negotiate my return."

There was a common driving force I came to recognize as the afternoon started to wind down. Dr. Puharich seemed as much a Truth seeker as me. He was such a down-to-earth and alluring guy. That's what made any suspicions about him uncomfortable because they ran counter to this soft-spoken man Jo and I had grown to really like—and in such a short amount of time. That being the case, I would have to reconcile my feelings about his involvement in any government cover-up.

As the long afternoon wrapped up, my thoughts drifted back to some parts of our conversation. I didn't think if he was involved in any government program around human-extraterrestrial hybridization, that he'd be talking to us about that. That seemed illogical. So maybe being as affable as he was, he was also just being truthful. From a scientific point of view I actually understood the desired outcome of cross-breeding to accelerate human potential. Thus, at least on a theoretical level, we seemed very much on the same page.

However, I was taken aback by his expression of having to *negotiate* his return. I kept asking myself, *what American attempts to negotiate his return?* Was 'negotiate' a slip of the tongue or was I just looking way too deeply into something that was completely innocent?

And finally, I had been at the precipice of telling him about the Palm

Springs encounter coming up soon, even inviting him, but on this basis of uncertainty, I couldn't. I wasn't ready. I needed more background about who he was and more time to build a friendship. In the meantime, I would see if I could locate any books he'd written.

At the end of the intriguing afternoon, the three of us hugged a warm goodbye. He told me that he'd get back to me to set up a meeting with Timothy. In a matter of days that's exactly what occurred.

It was a bright afternoon at Jo's house once again when Timothy knocked. We both greeted him. He was a charming young man in his early thirties. He was well-fed, medium height, fair-skin, a full head of dark hair and piercing eyes. His Scandinavian good looks filled out a solid, barrel-chested strong frame. However, nothing about him rang of extraterrestrial. He could pass as your neighbor. We sat around the dining room table and got to know each other for a little while.

"What do you plan to do with your abilities?" questioned Jo.

"I might move to the Midwest and work on unsolved crimes."

"That sounds like a worthwhile endeavor," Jo acknowledged.

"You'll certainly never be without work," I added.

Jo was anxious to get the wheels turning. "Timothy, would you want to see if you can tell us anything about what we have sealed up here?"

He kindly agreed. Jo slid a white business envelope across the table. He didn't touch it. He stared down upon it as though he could see through the envelope. He passed his hands over it. After studying it for less than a minute, he said, "This is a photo of a person. It's a woman. She has passed."

Jo confirmed this with a nod and asked, "Can you tell me anything more?"

"This was a young woman. Murdered. In a horrible way. She has no face."

Jo gasped and was very tearful. She nodded, acknowledging his accuracy. While she tried to speak, her voice trembled and became broken and whispered. "She was a friend. We were very close. She was shot in the face by a stalker with a shotgun."

"Oh Jo, I'm so sorry. She was a promising young woman."

I nudged a box of tissues to Jo. While she composed herself and dabbed her tears, I pulled a large carton from the floor and placed it on the table in front of Timothy. He studied the carton, then began staring down over the top of the box. After what seemed like only seconds, he looked at me. "It's a manuscript."

I nodded acknowledging that he was correct, but was shocked because the box was so oversized and irregular that it would have been impossible to know it was a manuscript. Impossible, that is, except for Timothy's abilities. He continued. "There's only one section in this manuscript that has continuous bold lettering. Maybe two full pages." I nodded again in agreement. "The last two lines are an error in this section."

I was flabbergasted. The minute detail and factual accuracy was really quite mindboggling. My eyes and expression must have conveyed my amazement. "Timothy! Impressive to say the least!"

I knew the paragraph and I knew the last two sentences. And I had known that they may have been incorrect. They concluded a section in an unfinished manuscript titled, *The Voice: A Journey through the Eyes of Spirit.* (Yes—this book you're holding!) I had been battling with myself trying to arrive at the most cogent interpretation which I ultimately got.

CHAPTER TWENTY-ONE

It was late night. I was catching up on some reading when Sid pulled up to the house. I parted the library curtains and saw him get out of his car. Before he could give his codified rap-rap, rap-a-tap-tap on the screen door, I was in the doorway staring at him decked out in his garb. His green beret was slanted to one side. His eminent WWII orange-tinted aviator goggles were strapped across his forehead. His face was slightly blurred through the haze of a lit cigarette clenched between his teeth and a smile. He could have been mistaken for Humphrey Bogart.

I was laughing. "Hey man! Welcome back! What brings the late-night Red Baron out?"

"Brother RC!" he muttered around his cigarette, then held it like a projectile and pressed it into the bottom of his shoe. He took the dead butt, wrapped it into a little piece of aluminum foil and dropped it into one of his leather jacket pockets. He smiled. "I was just out cruising the cosmos and did a low pass over your neighborhood when after taking a full reading on my instrument panel I noticed the electromagnetic field pulse on your street was undercharged, so I thought I'd park my lightship and create what we galaxy hoppers call perfect timing."

I stood there shaking my head—laughing with him at his elucidations. We gave each other a huge hug, our personal handshake and continuous smiles.

"My astro-traveling brother. Come in!"

"Figured you'd still be awake. What are you working on?"

"Reading Godfre Ray King's ascended masters series. I'm on *Unveiled Mysteries* now."

He chuckled. "Don't you ever give up? Guess I don't need to ask, eh? Isn't life just too complex a mystery to solve? We can never know God! We can only feel His presence like a breeze that passes through."

"So I'm a diehard. Hey—you joked about perfect timing, but I had the strangest thing happen earlier tonight. You've got to see this." I directed him to my bedroom. A lamp shade hung over the edge of my bed. It was comprised of more than 50 eyeglass lenses of various thicknesses all soldered together side-by-side. It was about the size of a basketball if you cut across and got rid of the bottom third. It hung down on a three-foot electrical cord woven through a silver chain. "Look at this reflection," I said. I stood him a couple feet from the wall where a shadow was cast from reflections off the lightbulbs through perhaps two of the lenses. "Does this image on the wall look familiar to you?"

He stood tall and cross-legged staring as though in a museum viewing a piece of art. His right elbow sat in the palm of his left hand. Studying the wall image, slowly massaging his chin, his expression instantly changed. "Richard. Richard. Richard. I see it."

"Tell me what you see."

"Hmm...now maybe this is my Christian upbringing, but it looks to me like dear Mother Mary on the right, in angelic form, holding Baby Jesus in her arms, also in angelic form."

"Sergeant Smith, that's what I see. I only discovered it tonight."

He remained baffled, shaking his head, his eyes refusing to leave the image. "That's...that's—"

"Coincidental?" I suggested.

"Intriguing for sure. How long has that lamp been hanging there?"

"Years."

"And you never saw this image before?"

"Not until two hours ago."

Sid ever-so-gently tapped the shade with an index fingernail which caused it to ever-so-slightly sway. The image immediately disappeared from the wall until it reappeared after the lamp resumed its original motionless position.

"Amazing, Richard. Really amazing."

"Look at this," I suggested, slightly unscrewing one of the three small bulbs under the shade. The image completely changed, unrecognizable from the prior sacred portrait on the wall.

Sid had a thought. "For this image to be as exact as it is, the filaments in the bulbs all have to work together to cast light through the precise few lenses out in front of it in exactly this position to create this image!"

"Exactly!" I declared. "What are the odds?"

"You know what pareidolia is, right?"

"Yes. Giving meaning to a random visual pattern," I explained.

"Yes. The mind tries to make sense out of what the eyes see."

"Sid, do you think this is pareidolia?" I wasn't sure.

"Richard, I think this is a gift. Since this lamp is free to swivel on its axis 360 degrees around on the wire, it may have taken years to capture this image on its present axis."

"Timing Sid. What timing."

"There are no coincidences, right? The mind of the Almighty knew you were ready to receive this gift so it became manifest into your reality at this very moment. The shade has probably been slowly turning on its axis, shifting the reflection closer and closer toward the opening on the wall as you moved closer and closer into a consciousness that would accept its significance."

I always enjoyed Sid's slice on life. "So, might this be that very *breeze* you were talking about just a few minutes ago?"

"Yes! That breeze entered your house without an open window."

I invited him to take a walk with me outside. Strolling curbside on the abandoned street, he stopped at a tall rose bush and snapped off a large red rose. As we continued walking, he tore off a big petal and started chewing on it.

He handed me one. "Vitamin C?"

I couldn't help but laugh. "No thanks. I got oranges in the house."

"Cool."

As he picked off more petals chewing and spitting them out, I began picking his brain. "Let me ask you something. I know you told me about being followed. I dismissed it as a remote possibility until my phone started clicking even more often now. I've been sharing with you much of what's been happening with me over the past few weeks and months."

"Lights in the sky. UFOs appearing. Close encounters—"

"Yes. This is the stuff of government intrigue, right?"

"Definitely."

"What do you think the odds are that my phone is bugged?"

"With me being followed, I'd say high probability. Your whole house could be bugged. There must be more going on you're not telling me."

"There is. I just didn't want to talk about it on the telephone."

I took in a deep breath of the late night early fall crisp air. There was a calming chill in it. I put my arm around him. He did the same. We strolled arm-and-shoulder down the middle of the street.

"So...more ships?"

"Yes. Like huge bright stars and they're getting closer and bigger and showing themselves to more people around me."

"Like who?"

"My neighborhood kids."

"No shit?"

"No shit!"

"That's wild! Who are they?"

"No idea. I just know they're here."

"What about Palm Springs on the twentieth? Is that still on?"

"Yes."

"It's only ten days away."

"I know, but I decided I'm not going out there alone. Would you?"

"Hell no! Especially in the middle of the night. Then who else is going?"

"You!"

He drew in a deep breath through his nose and exhaled. "I can't. You forgot. I have a commitment up north with the girls. I can't get out of it."

"Ugh—I did forget."

He cleared his throat, pulled a spare cigarette from behind his ear and lit it.

I always felt safe with Sid around. Our long-standing friendship was a bond like blood. There had always been an indescribable connection between us, like comrades in battle from eons of incarnations ago—our history, an unspoken, unbroken link that seemed to transcend time. Along with Dion, any of the three of us would have shed blood for the other.

"What about Dion?" he asked.

"I talked with him about this. He gave it a green light."

"Cool. And Jo?"

"The timeline can't work for her. But my friend Lorene—"

"The TV entertainer?"

"Yes." Lorene and I were just very close friends. "She told me she's always wanted to see a UFO and sincerely asked if she could come."

"Well, that'll be perfect. Who else?"

"Rick Hurst, Christopher and David."

"You'll have your own troop!"

"Yes. I feel good about their company. You'll be missed though."

Suddenly, I was overcome once again with that feeling. I stopped dead in my tracks in the middle of the abandoned road.

"What?" Sid asked with alarm in his tone. He could tell something was happening with me. He drew heavily on his cigarette. My eyes were glued to the southern moonlit sky. Sparce wisps of clouds stretched across the heavens backlit like a van Gogh painting. There was a tingling sensation coming through my entire body. Sid turned and faced me with his eyes bouncing between me and the endpoint of my gaze. "What?"

"I can't explain it, Sid." With unequivocal premonition I knew exactly what was going to happen. "Keep your eyes there," I said, pointing into the southern sky. "They're coming."

"How do you know?"

"I just know." I pointed. "Keep your focus there."

We stood side-by-side panning the southern sky. There were wide open areas between the clouds. Then from above the treetops many blocks away, fourteen vessels came from the south sailing silently in our direction. They were very low, perhaps five hundred feet above the tree line. They approached like geese in V-formation without a sound, but there was no mistaking it. These were not geese. Moonlight reflected off curved surfaces of the vessels while they silently glided across the sky. Sid and I were at a loss for words. The vessels soared majestically almost directly over us and off into northern darkness.

CHAPTER TWENTY-TWO

After Sid left, I returned to the house. Sprawled out on the Chinese rug with a pillow under my neck and staring at glowing logs in the fireplace, my thoughts also happened to be ablaze. I never observed anybody following me and I didn't think my phone would be bugged.

Shadow crawled up in between my long-outstretched legs, released a comforting meow and settled in. But comfort was not what my life seemed to be about. *What was that squadron of vessels I had witnessed?* If they were the Greys, I reasoned, maybe that's who flew over. Maybe that's what all of them are. I knew I was not able to tell by merely looking at a craft whether it was benevolent, so all I had to offer myself was deeper intuition and greater discernment. Had all these recent events had anything to do with my childhood encounter?

My eyes focused on the dancing flames as my body relaxed into quiet breathing. A slow and steady breath in. Blow out. Slow breath in…blow out. It was just after one in the morning. I was beat, but I couldn't settle my thoughts. Sid's paranoia played over and over in my head. It seemed like such a ridiculous assumption that my house and phone would be bugged. However, I was perseverating on that notion.

A shot of adrenaline raced through me. I bolted around the house in search of a possible hidden microphone or camera. I looked under countertops, tables, in lamp shades, hanging pictures, hunting for anything suspicious or something that appeared to have been moved or was obviously out of place.

I found nothing.

I sat down on the sofa thinking just how paranoia can permeate the spirit. My house being bugged may not have been so farfetched I concluded. I knew that a microphone might be impossible to locate within the house—few people are versed in such matters—but maybe it wasn't necessary to be an electronics genius I thought. This spurred an idea.

The only lights on in the house were in the living room. I turned them off and lit a candle. I put on some soft music, removed my sneakers and tiptoed into the laundry room. I put on leather work gloves, swept a hammer off a shelf and picked up an old broken pane of glass beside the clothes dryer. I stopped in the kitchen, picked up a thick plastic trash bag, brought the oversized plastic waste basket tub into the living room, spread the bag inside and silently set everything up beside the telephone on the large Chinese rug. I carefully and without a sound placed the pane of glass into the barrel and tiptoed to the front door where I removed one glove. I knocked loudly on my dead-bolted front door.

"Hold on!" I shouted back into the living room to myself. "Coming!" I threw the deadbolt on the front door then opened it. I kicked the screen door open and let it slam shut. "Hey hey! What do you want?" I pushed closed the interior front door and pleaded with the imagined intruder. "Who are you? What the—who the hell are...hey! Hey! Hey! HEY!"

A mock scuffle ensued with myself. I placed my hand over my mouth, muffling my pleas and yells, releasing the glove just long enough to get out one final terrorizing quick scream. I knocked a metal chair against the wall sending it crashing onto the rug. I approached the waste basket, moaning and sounding frightened for my life, and threw the hammer against the glass inside the barrel. The sound of my muffled screams along with exploding glass and shattered fragments falling into the barrel filled the room with cacophony. The last pieces of glass trickled to silence as I released one final gasp of air and dropped to the floor in a thud. Only the sound of soft background music was heard in the living room.

I reasoned that if my place had interior video surveillance, my escapade would surely have been caught on camera. Anybody monitoring would care less about such antics. However, if there was only interior audio surveillance, anyone monitoring might think I had been murdered. I presumed this might be enough to generate a welfare check by a phone call or a police car drive-by to merely confirm if there was reason for concern.

I ran to the library where the curtains were only parted by inches. The room was dark. I sat far back from the window in complete darkness peering out to the street and wondering if my bait would catch a fish. After ten minutes I gave up. The telephone didn't ring and not even one car passed by the house. With no apparent response indicated, I assumed no cameras and no interior audio monitoring. The next logical step to rule out surveillance was to see if perhaps only my phone was tapped, thus carrying on the same performance.

So, I set up the same scenario in the living room. This time my plan was to knock over the telephone so the ruckus would be heard through the receiver. Once accomplished, if there was a response by means of a phone call once the receiver was put back on the hook, I knew I would be catching a whale. I imagined if I was doing the monitoring. The logical deduction from anyone listening would be concern about my safety. To confirm if I was dead or alive, all that would be needed would be to place one call to the house to see if anyone responded and who picked up the phone. I reasoned if there was a response, so as not to give away true surveillance, all the caller would have to do is hang up. If I answered, it would be assumed I was at least alive. If a stranger answered, voilà! It would be perceived that my life might certainly be in danger.

The barrel was ready. I knocked the phone receiver out of the cradle and began the mock fight with myself. I hollered a few desperate screams with a glove over my mouth within a couple feet of the phone, smashed what remained of the large pieces of glass inside the barrel, fought with myself, moaned loudly, knocked the metal chair over again and let out a final quick scream into my glove right next to the phone. Then silence prevailed. I waited half a minute, then carefully placed the receiver back into its cradle.

Sitting on the floor waiting to see if I would hit a homerun, I removed my gloves with my gaze fixed on the telephone only inches from my face. I waited. Ten seconds. Twenty seconds. The room was quiet except for soft music. Then the telephone rang. I looked at my watch. It was 1:30 in the morning. I gulped. This was stupendous. I waited. Although my worst possible fear was materializing, I wasn't going to rush into answering. I also couldn't help thinking what a terrible irony this would be if Sid was calling. However, I knew Sid never called this late. If I was right and my phone was bugged, this caller was expecting me to be seriously injured or perhaps dead. The phone rang a second time and again I waited.

In the middle of the third ring I answered, shaking to my very core. I waited a couple seconds, then spoke in a whisper.

"Hello."

Nobody responded.

I waited.

"Hello!" I repeated, then waited a couple more seconds.

Again, no response.

Then I spoke. "Dead men can't answer phones, can they? Dead men don't talk, do they? Why are you doing this to me?" I pleaded. "Who are you?"

I heard a click. The phone went dead.

I couldn't believe I had just pulled this off. Confirmation was now rock solid. At one-thirty in the morning there was no such thing as coincidence. What were the odds of predicting this event with the telephone ringing and nobody responding? I was concerned by this confirmation. I also knew if Sid's car was being monitored, surely that was happening to me. I just hadn't noticed.

Staring at the phone with growing anger, the dial tone came on. Since this likely confirmed government involvement, that could only mean I was on to something that obviously represented either a threat to the government or a mystery a government agency itself was hoping to solve by means of surveillance. Otherwise, why bother? I was small fish so why waste time with me?

"If you'd like to make a call, please hang up and dial again or ask your operator—" came the recorded voice through the receiver lying on the rug. I placed the receiver back into the cradle and started pacing the living room. The reality of the situation slowly was sinking in. My phone was bugged. My house was not. With each stride back and forth a rage progressively built up. I found myself pacing between the living room and library. The feeling of someone knowing my every conversation, my thoughts, my private life and business was really reprehensible. It was disturbing. Invasive. I was pissed. My pounding fist on the desk sent a jar full of pens and pencils dancing. I couldn't get past how inexcusable this whole thing was.

"You bastards!" I wailed in anger. "You bastards!"

I grew raging mad. I could feel my entire body overheating. I knew that everything about this began from the meeting at Charlie Martin's place, precisely as Sid had claimed. I couldn't shake the feeling of being trespassed upon. Wire-tapped no less! The sense of intrusion was overwhelming. A final twist of my body and a scream of madness in the darkness of my library caught me unaware of the telephone cord. I tripped over it which ensnared a pile of books on my desk that went flying with me. I reached for the desk to catch myself, but more books and files went flying onto the floor. The final book to land beside me was Pastor Jack's Bible. Laying breathless flat out across the rug, my thoughts were as dark as the room.

"Son of a bitch!"

Uninjured, rolling over and laying on my back, I caught my breath. From the quiet I could hear a distant whisper. I thought it was my panting, so I continued to quiet myself, calming down, breathing more easily, recovering from my outburst.

Listening in the silence of the room, a distant Voice spoke. "For—" I heard so feathered and faint that I was unable to distinguish anything further. I stilled my thoughts and listened attentively. A perfectly audible telepathic Voice began to softly speak. *"Forgive and love."*

I repeated it. "Forgive…and…love."

I believed what I was hearing—forgive and love the interlopers. Of course! I just couldn't do that though.

"Forgive and love," the Voice repeated distinctly.

I understood the message. I saw the wisdom. I realized that to harbor such ill feelings made me the victim. Intellectually—I got it. I knew that. And the more I thought about it, the more I remembered the same Truth being part of Adele's wisdom: *forgive everybody for everything*. I was emotionally stuck once again. I could not dismiss this egregious violation.

"Ohhh! Don't ask me to do that," I protested under my breath, challenging the greater wisdom. This felt just over the top.

I marched into the living room, upset and conflicted by the challenge to forgive. "I can't do that. You can't ask me to do that," I again uttered into the open living room air. At that exact moment a lightbulb in a lamp blew out in a quiet poof. I turned on the overhead light, walked over to the lamp and saw something etched into the lightbulb. I unscrewed it and peered down upon it. Burned across the entire inside top and side portions of the bulb was what appeared to be the body and expansive outspread wings of a white butterfly. I was truly stunned. For whatever reason, I instinctively held it up to the ceiling light, thereby backlighting the bulb and the image. Instantly a spectacular new image emerged. Its left outstretched wing looked like an arm extended up at eleven o'clock, the right at one o'clock. You could kind of make out a figure's head slightly hung to the left with its unmistakable full-length scraggly brown hair hanging down below its shoulders. It had the striking resemblance and hallmark features of Jesus. He just wasn't on the cross. *Was this once again pareidolia?*

I clutched this precious gift in my hand and understood the need to forgive. It was the same old hurdle repeating itself. I could see that. I was in a struggle.

With such gentility and the warmth of compassion, the Voice whispered, **"But what have you taught the children?"**

CHAPTER TWENTY-THREE

It was Saturday morning when Jo and I stood around her backyard playing with Anna and Kiba. On that particular day the wind had picked up and was blowing leaves and debris everywhere. There had also been a notable earthquake a few days earlier that didn't only cause Jo's house to rattle, but shook her. We were discussing the recent quake.

"I could hear the frame of my house sound like it tweaked with a loud crack," she said.

Jo's hair kept flying across her face. I took some strands away from her mouth. "We can't worry about these earthquakes," I said. "There's nothing we can do about it unless we move out of state. And something else I should share with you. You know the presence of this Off-Planet Intelligence is persistent. They've even revealed their vessels to the kids. My hunch is that your house could come crashing down with you and me in it and we'd be found safe outside wondering how we ever got out." I pointed skyward. "They would just remove us from this house. It may sound strange, but I feel protected by their presence, Jo. They're all around as you can see. They're watching what's going on. Don't stress over this. And besides with gusts like today there's a better chance of your house blowing away!"

My comforting thoughts seemed to ease her tension We wrapped up our morning, hugged and kissed goodbye. She headed to the backyard guest house to meet a patient for a counseling session and I decided I'd go off on an adventure. It had been quite some time since our meeting with Dr. Puharich, so I thought this would be a perfect time to see if I could locate any of his books. I hightailed down to the Fairfax District on the east side of Hollywood to the used bookstore division of the Bodhi Tree off Melrose Avenue. Jo and I planned to meet up later at her place.

Once parked at the used bookstore I flew out of my car, leaped over the three short concrete steps up to the landing into the Bodhi Tree and raced over to the metaphysical section. I started eyeballing book after book alphabetically listed by author's last name. Finally, I spotted the spine of one book I was seeking and grabbed it: *A Journal of the Mystery of Uri Geller* by Andrija Puharich. I sensed this might be my lucky day. However, despite my exhaustive search, book after book, shelf after shelf, finding no other Puharich books, I decided to try other categories. Row after row I could not find another book by him.

After a good hour of painstaking searches, I was at a loss and decided to throw in the towel. I felt lucky to have at least found one book. I started walking down the long hallway to get to the cashier, but as I passed the stockroom, the door was wide open. The lights were off, but on a quick glance I saw a long wooden worktable on which must have been hundreds of books. From the hallway I saw they were neatly stacked about 30-40 books tall, column after column, side by side. I peaked in to see if any staff was present to get permission to go inside, but no one was there. I was extremely hesitant to just walk in as that was conduct not typical of me. But I felt an unexplained nudging which overpowered my sense of trespassing.

Standing by the end of the table, my eyes fell upon the first four stacks of books. I scanned across those laying on top. I didn't touch any of them. Sitting on top of one of four piles at the very end was *The Sacred Mushroom*. If I felt downright lucky finding the Uri book, I sensed that this serendipitous moment was a gift beyond luck, beyond chance, beyond any statistical odds. I vacillated between believing this was one extraordinary miracle, or that there was far more here than meets the eye. The scientist in me rationalized this could have been a materialization by Hoova. However, deeper mindfulness was suggesting this might be the work of my Master Teacher. Pondering all considerations, this seemed to be a living example right out of my lucid dream: *Spirit works within coincidence which is our way of reminding you we are with you. This element is Divinely inspired to better serve mankind.*

I removed the book from the top of the pile and walked out into the hallway clutching the two Puharich books. I reviewed what had just occurred. All facets of what unfolded would have to have been aligned perfectly because of what would have been required for all of it to come together. Typically, I never would have walked into an unattended stockroom. Yet, I was compelled. Respectful of the bookstore, I would never have touched or pilfered through any books without permission. Thereby, it would have required that this book be located at the end of the table and on top.

The whole incident just took my breath away. Thinking more about it, further validation from my lucid dream came to mind: *That's how Divine action occurs. Through thought. Through you. Living this wisdom will unveil lines of synchronicity....*"

After some incidental errands, I headed back to Jo's. I walked in and was given a warm greeting. However, Anna and Kiba were conspicuously missing at the front door where they would typically greet me. Instead, they were hiding in a corner of the living room unusually demure. Their happy ears usually raised high were lowered and retracted.

Jo initiated conversation as I walked in. "I have to tell you something very strange that happened after you left."

"And I have one to tell you," I said, plunking down the two Puharich books on her kitchen counter for her to view which I would later explain.

"After you left," she said, "I locked the dogs in the house. It was so windy that I didn't want them playing in the yard while I saw my client. Once I put them in the house, I deadbolted the doors so the wind couldn't possibly blow them open. About fifteen minutes into my session, I see them running all around the yard. I couldn't figure it out. I assumed when I threw the deadbolt it must not have engaged. After the session I went back to the door and tried to push it open, but it was deadbolted! I had to use my key to unlock it. I checked the second door and it too was deadbolted. How could this have happened?"

"I know exactly how."

"You do?"

"Remember our conversation earlier this morning?"

"No."

"I suggested that in case of an earthquake, they," I pointed up, "*they* could just pluck us from this house for our safety if it was collapsing after an earthquake."

She immediately got it. The dogs were used as confirmation of what I had told her. Both dogs were chowhounds, but apparently were traumatized enough that they stopped eating for a couple days from fear of what they could not understand. I felt sad that they had been used to make a point.

In the meantime, I pursued reading of Dr. Puharich's book about Uri. When I hit pages 193-194, what he had written put a reassuring smile on my face. He witnessed his black Labrador retriever Wellington go from the doorway of the house to suddenly being down the driveway in the time his telephone went from the first ring to the second ring. He wrote that Wellington had been 'translocated.'

CHAPTER TWENTY-FOUR

The Palm Springs date arrived. Despite the directive to come alone for the encounter, I could not take the risk. I had firmed up among my friends who would participate. Because of the timeline, it was impossible for Jo to attend.

I picked up Lorene on the afternoon of Saturday, October 19, 1985 for whatever would unfold that night at 2 a.m. We headed east out of Los Angeles.

She turned to me. "What time is something supposed to happen?"

"I got this feeling that it's between midnight tonight and six in the morning. However, Christopher telephoned me to say he received a telepathic message directly from Immoway."

"About the time?"

"Yes."

Lorene looked at me with the same amazement I felt after Christopher had relayed that message. "He said exactly two in the morning."

"Oh boy. I'm nervous."

"About what?"

She bent over toward me with an innocent schoolgirl giggle. "I didn't pack enough for an abduction!"

"Come on!"

"You don't think there's anything we should be worried about, right?"

"My heart's beating a little faster than I'd like it to, but I feel safe. We'll just move cautiously."

"Cautiously? Cautiously! That's not reassuring me!"

"Look, it's the unknown. I feel like I'm walking a bit in the dark so I'll depend on intuition. I just have to do my best not to operate out of fear. That's been my challenge. So maybe we can help each other."

"Deal."

"Like I told the kids, they could have carried me off a long time ago if that was their intention. Also, Dion, Rick, Christopher and David will join us. My feeling is there's safety in numbers. What do you think?"

She was such a natural clown. She became quite animated with crossed eyes and a goofy smile. She pushed her cheek out with her tongue and stared at me. It got both of us laughing hysterically. Her smile consumed both her expression and a mouthful of teeth as bright as ivory keys popping into view on a Steinway piano. I loved the joy she inspired at every opportunity. Her playfulness. Her innocence. Even wonder about life. She put me right there with her like a kid in a candy store.

"Richard, I'm really excited! You know I've never seen a UFO. Will your parents be there?"

"No. They're still back in Syracuse, but we'll be able to stay in their home. It's vacant so we'll all be comfortable. My sister Joy lives two blocks away with her husband and my niece Anoeschka who you already met a while ago. I explained to them all about the telepathic invitation."

"You had mentioned being monitored. What do you think?"

"Whoever's monitoring, well, it's just outside my control. There's nothing we can do about it. So, we can only forgive them for their ignorance, try to be fearless and agree it is what it is."

We arrived at the family Palm Springs home where Anoeschka was relaxing during her school vacation. At my suggestion she had already started setting up the house for the guests. Beautiful broad candles with low flames illuminated the great room. Soft, soothing, melodic music filled the air. A variety of oversized pillows were welcoming across the living room carpet. The large, rambling, white brick, mid-century style house wound its way through three thousand feet of terraces, patios and gardens. It was a balmy evening and a slight breeze moved through open windows that gave life to flickering candles. By 8 p.m. everybody had arrived. The ambiance was tranquil and welcoming. We waited for whatever event was to occur, but no one including me could have anticipated what was about to unfold.

Time marched on. No one was paying attention to the music or the time. Lorene and Dion were buried in a stack of pillows and conversation. Christopher and David were on the carpet table-tipping like Adele. Rick and I were debating the probabilities and improbabilities of amorphous life.

I kept glancing at my watch, anxious over how slowly time was passing. The many candles in the living room, finally giving off only a soft flickering orange glow, seemed to have melted down to about the same level as our energy. Fatigue was contagious.

While I was in the kitchen, Lorene meandered over and tapped her watch. She took hold of my arm and we quietly and inconspicuously meandered across the living room to the large sliding glass doors. At this late hour many guests were asleep right where they were last chatting.

"What time is it?" I whispered.

"Exactly two o'clock."

I slowly slid open one of the doors and we exited onto the back patio. We headed over to the pool area where an expanse of the sky came sharply into view. The heavens were filled with countless sparkling stars on this clear night. We could hear Anoeschka laughing with Christopher further away on a separate terrace—the only other two seemingly still awake. The sound of crickets and chasing Mockingbirds abruptly stopped. An uncanny silence prevailed except for the onset of a low frequency hum.

"Do you hear that?" I queried.

She nodded in agreement.

We reached the mid-area beside the pool and from that vantage point the view completely opened. Immediately we could see two vessels in the sky perhaps half a mile away slowly traversing from the right to the left halfway between us and the horizon. One was only a short distance in the lead fully encased in an intense red glow. The second vessel was lit up like New Year's Eve floating across the lower dark sky fully illuminated from within and without. It gave off sparkling white light spires all around the periphery that shot straight up and high like glistening stalagmites. We could not take our eyes off what we were witnessing.

"Richard, it looks like a brilliant crystal chandelier."

I knew exactly what it looked like. "I see the floating crown of a king."

"Richard! Yes! I see that too!"

"This is extraordinary, Lorene."

"I've never seen anything like this."

I was gobsmacked. Its presence was just dazzling. Lorene drew herself close to me as I put my arm around her shoulder. We were nestled together in awe of what we were witnessing. I wanted to capture every single aspect of this magnificent heavenly scene gliding across the sky, but it was almost as if my mind struggled to grasp what it was witnessing.

"Lorene, this thing is huge! It could be a mothership!"

My peripheral vision caught her nodding in agreement. Her eyes also never left the sky. The two vessels held the same steady pace as they traversed and were about to fade into the dark of night. Just then guests were stirred and began joining us. It was too late. Hearing the commotion Christopher and Anoeschka joined from another terrace. They too missed it. I was so spellbound from what I had witnessed I didn't even know what to say. Lorene explained what we'd seen. I tried to recover from the shock. The image of the massive sovereign vessel played over and over in my head.

Hearing Lorene's description, Rick was overwhelmed. "Incredible!" he whispered, wishing all of them had come out in time.

Guests decided to remain outside for a while under the warm night sky to see if something more might develop. Once everyone found a recliner, Lorene turned to me and asked, "Do you think they'll return?"

"I really don't know," I confessed.

She laid down beside the pool and called to Dion. "Would you please hold my hand?" He ambled over, laid down beside her and held her hand. "Does anyone hear that hum?" she asked.

"It's a warble," Dion said.

With a protective arm around Anoeschka, Christopher acknowledged, "I hear it."

David couldn't hear it.

"I can hear it!" Anoeschka whispered in a shaky voice of excitement.

Rick didn't understand what we were talking about. "Hear what you guys?"

"That hum!" Christopher categorically confirmed.

I heard it and could almost nail the frequency. Our audiometric pure tone generating equipment at the clinic could test as low as 125 Hz. It was lower than that, but not by very much. After twenty minutes the only ones who could hear the mysterious hum were Dion and Lorene, and only if they continued to hold hands. It was very strange. No one understood the dynamics behind it. The sound was localized coming from somewhere above the house.

By 3 a.m. when not even an airplane was seen in the sky, everyone returned to the house for the night. I had accepted the extraterrestrial invitation both fearfully and curiously. While I was immensely intrigued by the evening's events, there was a feeling that something much more was to have happened. A landing? Maybe direct communication to my group? Had I come alone, would I have been invited aboard?

After the guests settled back down or were asleep, I happened to run into Anoeschka in the kitchen. She wanted to ask me a bunch of questions about the event so I suggested we return to the back patio to avoid disturbing our guests. Once on the patio a physical sensation overtook me. It felt as though I had walked into some kind of active electromagnetic field. My skin and hair on my body seemed alive. I looked straight up.

A long elliptical cloud was positioned maybe a thousand feet above the house. Anoeschka took careful note of it with me. It appeared to run three miles long, a half mile wide and gave off an ever-so-slight blue glow. The longest portion of the cloud ran east and west; the width ran north and south. We were under the southwest wing of it.

As our eyes adapted to the night sky, we were able to study it more carefully. A dry ice-like vapor around the entire periphery of the cloud mass rolled downward and dissipated quickly. I looked at wide-eyed Anoeschka and we both agreed that the golden vessel was almost certainly now in this cloud. We stood there viewing this mysterious artifact, transfixed by what we were witnessing. Christopher and David who had been in the living room heard our quiet commotion and joined us back on the patio. We four stood motionless when Christopher confirmed the same intuitive feelings Anoeschka and I had.

"Wow!" Christopher said. "This cloud is hiding the mothership!"

Anoeschka started shivering uncontrollably. Christopher placed his light jacket around her shoulders. It was her nerves that ran to the core of her not knowing their intentions. "What if these are fallen angels?" she whispered.

I had been dealing with my own fear. I wasn't ready for a religious history lesson to top it off. "It's okay Anoeschka. No harm will come from any of this,"

I said reassuringly, wondering if I needed to hear these very words to quell my own fears.

All eyes were glued to the sight above. We witnessed multiple UFOs with no illumination start to drop down below the cloud, hover silently, and shoot across the waxing crescent moonlit sky and disappear. A slight breeze filled the air, yet the cloud remained motionless, even in the presence of little gusts of wind.

The four of us took a seat. From our recliners laid out flat we continued peering into the sky. We were simply astonished at the activity. The same kind of vessels appeared from out of the darkness, arrived below the cloud, hovered, then rose up into the cloud. They all were oval-saucer shaped, appeared to be perhaps thirty feet wide with a matte-steely dullness. Docking maneuvers continued with multiple vessels coming and going until Anoeschka headed into the house to go to sleep.

Sometime later Christopher noticed that it appeared I wasn't my calm self. He was right. I was wrestling with disappointment. He turned to me with a furrowed brow. "You okay? What's going on?"

"Something isn't right. I don't know. Something more or different was supposed to happen."

"It's happening! Look up!"

"No. Not docking maneuvers. I can't explain it. I don't even know exactly what. Just a feeling."

He read the frustration in my expression. "Let's go in the house and speak to Immoway at the table." He swung his arm around me and we headed back into the house.

We sat on the floor opposite each other with the light wooden piano bench between us. Christopher had become skilled at table-tipping. He and David were getting quite proficient at it. Christopher placed his hands on the bench, closed his eyes, took in long, slow, deep breaths and released them. I put my hands on it with my fingertips almost touching his. It started rocking back and forth. I couldn't tell if Christopher was tipping it or if it was doing so by itself—like Adele.

"Immoway is here," Christopher whispered.

"Were you the ones who we witnessed here earlier?" I asked. The bench moved from flat on the floor to tipping three times in my direction, then rested back on the floor. That was *yes*. This whole set-up felt absurd. Communicating with a commander of a ship from another star system through my parent's piano bench? *What!?* However, I witnessed Adele do the same through her kitchen table. Was this any crazier? I was ready for anything. Besides, Christopher had been the one through Immoway who nailed the exact time for my encounter, so who was I to judge?

Our upper bodies rocked in unison with movement of the bench. Our breathing became synchronized. Soon, his face took on an entirely different expression. Perspiration formed on his brow, his mouth dropped open and dry, and he rolled his head around with his eyes closed and flickering. My attention was fixed on this gentle soul who was about to experience his first direct channeling between us.

"Richard. Immoway is asking me to tell you we don't need the bench to channel this."

Had Immoway read my mind? Christopher's body jerked and spasmed as he felt a strange and wonderful surge of energy come through him. He knew how to go with the flow. Only a small portion of the whites of his eyes could be seen between the quivering slits of his eyelids. He remained calm and tranquil and allowed the deepest flow within to reach his lips which began to twitch with electrical charge. Then Christopher, as a channel, spoke in words not originating from within his own thought pattern. His inflection and tone were completely foreign to me.

"The event was intended just for you," he—Immoway—said. "It was not what you thought because it was not who should have been here."

There was a long silence as my thoughts seemed to sink down into a very somber place. I had already realized my mistake. It was too late to correct the past. I was ashamed how fear steered my decision making. I felt embarrassed—maybe even humiliated. What had I done? Christopher hadn't known that I was originally invited there alone because I had told only my family and Sid in confidence.

"Richard, we are here to assist man in a great transition. It is a time for change in the world…on the Earth. We are here to help. Don't be scared."

The message resonated. To some I might have appeared courageous around my encounters. However, living inside was that boy of nine still shaking in the arms of a Being of Light. It was the Figure back then; a cloud and a vessel tonight. Neither a threat. It was apparent how transformation out of fear could be tortuously slow. The old Richard was dying, yes, but a gruelingly slow death.

Was Immoway and his group part of Hoova or some other species? I hadn't even known who invited me to the encounter. According to Dr. Puharich as reported to him by Hoova, there are twenty-four civilizations involved in our coexistence. In the 1980s the risk of abduction was just too big. Couldn't this Off-Planet Intelligence understand that? My thin cotton shirt was clinging like a magnet to my ever-sweating chest. I had to get a grip on myself.

Christopher and I took in simultaneous deep breaths and slowly released them in unison. It seemed we were in perfect harmony. A force pushed its way through him. His lips quivered again. He will later explain that he welcomed the use of his physical body to allow the wisdom of Immoway to speak, even though he had no recall of the channeling.

"When will I get to see you, Immoway?" I asked.

In a voice unknown to me, in quite an unusually resonant baritone quality, Immoway said, "We vibrate at a different frequency than you. It would be difficult for you to understand us. We are Light Beings. We live by direct emanations of Light. Only under certain conditions can we both come into physical contact. But soon with changes that are coming, we will be able to work together. Move past your fear so you'll recognize those from the heavens who have held true to the Greater Plan."

Christopher sat for half a minute in what appeared to be a deep trance state; then exhausted, dropped backwards onto the pillows. I got thinking. Yes. Fear. The barrier. Holding trust for someone or something I didn't understand was a very high bar. Was such conquest of fear going to come next week? Next month? Next year? Exactly when would I decide enough is enough? Where was that transformation I set out for?

I let Christopher rest and returned to the pool area where docking maneuvers were ongoing. I was alone. I laid back in a recliner where I would spend the entire night under the cloud watching the activity. I was grateful for the opportunity to have been one of the witnesses to this bold extraterrestrial display, but in truth, I had been looking for something so much deeper. While Immoway's communication had been reassuring, it didn't answer a single question for me; something that would address the mystery over my childhood encounter or how I could establish a clearer connection to the Divine.

The cool night air sailed across my face. It felt good. I stopped beating myself up and forgave myself at least for the time being. I was at peace. I breathed in a huge sigh of relief. I wasn't even afraid. I got it. I no longer thought I was going to be abducted. Even if I was wrong, I was resigned to it being just fine. I'm sure I would have learned something new. My old maxim came to mind. *You cannot fear the very spiritual path you seek.* That rang so true now. My eyes started to close of their own volition. I pulled up a checkered wool blanket to cover myself—the one my parents had been saving from when I was such a young boy. In minutes I was asleep.

The following morning, we found ourselves a little dazed. It wasn't the lack of sleep as much as the impact of being witnesses to the events. Before we returned to Los Angeles, we shared our observations. What we all saw as a group was fully consistent person to person. However, there were no real conclusions drawn about the purpose behind it all—only deeper mysteries. What had been their purpose? Who were they and where were they from? Why did they reveal so many vessels and show us docking maneuvers? Was there to be a second invitation?

I felt like I should know, but I had no answers.

CHAPTER TWENTY-FIVE

After a relaxing and healing meditation completed on my living room rug, my body felt renewed. Through the windows I could see it was a beautiful day. I threw on shorts and a t-shirt and walked barefoot out into the front yard garden among the last of the remaining fall flowers. The scent of night blooming jasmine wafted here and there along my trek across the flourishing Kentucky Bluegrass. The high uncut grass was cold and refreshing under my warm feet.

On this early sunny afternoon in Los Angeles, Johnny and Maddie already returned from church and were playing on their front lawn across the street. When they spotted me, we exchanged warm waves of acknowledgement.

I continued pacing across the grass under shade from the pines above. Throughout my life I had approached spiritual matters like any good scientist worth his weight. Objectivity. Measurement. Repeatability. They were all the rigors of conditioning that I was unfortunately still applying to my spiritual journey. I never had any fears in science or of science. It had been a solid foundation and reality on which I built a career. But spiritual endeavors held fear for me because of indoctrination and unknown consequences. What I was coming to see was that I needed to let go of objectivity, measurement and proof. With Spirit, you close your eyes and *feel*. What you feel is not in the head. It's in the heart and can't be seen. That was my challenge—opening my heart.

As I sauntered over to a recliner with a clear spirit and pure heart, I did something I had never done before. Silently, in my mind, I spoke to the garden as if it could hear me. I addressed all living things in it and beyond.

"To all life in this garden, know that on this afternoon I only bring you love. And God, if You are really here, know that I bring You the same love. Please let the animals of Your garden know that I will not harm them in any way. Let them know that on this day I only bring them love."

I suddenly felt I had entered some special garden, a sacred space as I gingerly traversed the grass with care not to step on even an ant. I took a seat in the recliner beneath the two huge pines towering over me. There was an unexplainable transparency about me. A peacefulness. A connectedness. In every way it was as if I was at last coming naked before God.

I laughed at the simplicity of my very first, direct, focused, intentional talk to God. I melded into the recliner with the backrest at forty-five degrees. I watched two Monarch butterflies zigzag their way to a flower. Their black, yellow and orange hues magnificently contrasted against the dark green grass beneath me. One last pink rose was still in bloom. I smiled and was glad Sid hadn't found it. Bees searching for pollen hovered around the rose. Birds harkened interest to one another somewhere in the dense pines far above.

My small front yard seemed to be a little piece of paradise. The sun of the day trickled down through the expanse of overhead branches. I closed my eyes. There was a profoundly powerful inner stillness within me. Silently, in my mind, I extended love to all the creatures around me, knowing they couldn't hear me, but wanting to do so just the same. It was a new and freeing feeling. In all the years in that home or anywhere I'd been, I had never done this.

Suddenly with tremendous volume that filled my entire head, I heard a Voice as clearly as the giggles from the children across the street. *"Would you like me to bring you a butterfly?"*

The Voice was gentle yet commanding and sounded like it was coming from someone standing inside of me versus some external source. It was not my voice. I blinked my eyes a few times, stared straight ahead and didn't move. I remained speechless. After a few seconds I looked around the yard for the source of the Voice because it was so perfectly clear, but I saw no one except Johnny and Maddie still playing across the street.

"Would you like me to bring you a butterfly?" repeated the gentle Voice, as audibly and magnificently as a father might ask his young son.

The resonance of the Voice, its depth of penetration through me and the clarity of the words all mystified me. This Voice was distinctly initiating conversation with me, like when I was at the Good Earth Restaurant, but something was different now. Was it me or was it the Voice? The tone of the Voice, its articulation, diction, fluency, pitch and resonance commanded my attention in an almost sacred manner. This was brand new. Every cell of my being resonated with the beauty of this Voice. I searched for what to say, what to do. Doubt, disobey or challenge I would not.

"Would you like me to bring you a butterfly?"

"Yes. Yes!" I quickly acknowledged, enamored and smiling with delight, intrigued by such a proposition.

"Would you like me to place him on the big toe of your left foot?"

I had to blink a few more times. *This is crazy. Now this is really crazy!* I started giggling. "Why yes. Yes! Sure," I replied. "That would be fine!"

Stupefied, but not disbelieving any of this for even a moment—that lesson had been learned—I looked around for the appearance of the promised butterfly. I saw the same gorgeous Monarch butterflies roaming around the grass and some white ones hovering around the flowerbed. I wondered which beautiful one might be coming to me.

In just seconds, from a distance, a plain, nondescript, timeworn butterfly with weather-beaten torn wings approached low over the grass. It swept past me from the right and into the air, then just as promised, it landed on the big toe of my left foot. From its perch on my toe it stared at me with its beady black eyes. A sudden broad smile stretched across my face. I was in true wonderment.

"Ohhh!" I muttered on a long exhalation. It seemed I could sense this butterfly's heart of compassion.

"Would you like me to bring you a bee from my garden and place it on the big toe of your right foot?" asked the Voice.

Immediately, I was infused with fear. Since childhood I had been dealing with apiphobia—a fear of bees. I remembered the terror from a day when I was about eleven years old. It was summer of 1956, a warm and pleasant afternoon much like this autumn day with the Voice. My mother and I were gardening in shorts and t-shirts. Suddenly, we heard an ominous roar coming from the sky. We had never heard anything like it. Before we knew it, a brown cloud had descended and we were amidst a frenzy of tens of thousands of bees. We hadn't taken our first step when hundreds of bees began dropping from the cloud with several landing in my mother's hair. She beat them away the best she could, but the more she flailed the greater they frenzied.

I remember screaming. "Mama! Run!"

I grabbed her hand and tried to pull her along with me, but she was immobilized by her fear. I looked on in horror. Remarkably, the bees were not after me. I knew we had to reach the safety of the screened porch. My mother's life was in peril. She was anaphylactic. One sting could have impaired her breathing, or worse, stopped her heart. Haphazardly beating a path through the brown haze of clustering bees and still a distance from the porch, my mother stumbled and fell. I was certain I could see blood all about her bare arms and legs and face and the thought horrified me.

She looked up at me, hollering, but her voice was weak, almost inaudible above the deafening roar of the bees.

"Go Richie! Go!" she screamed, sitting on the grass, flailing.

"No Mom! Get up! Get up!" I tugged relentlessly on her arm. "Get up!"

I helped her onto her feet. Standing would put her at risk so she stooped over at my height. We began to run. She cried hysterically as she swatted bees from her body. The screened porch was close. Sweat ran down our foreheads.

We made it inside the porch. She collapsed to the floor paralyzed in fear, moaning and dazed, covered with broken fragments of bees all about her skin.

"Would you like me to bring you a bee from my garden and place it on the big toe of your right foot?" the Voice asked again.

Fear raced through every pore in my body. I recognized I could kick the butterfly off my toe, jump off the recliner and run, but I'd be running from myself. I looked around and indeed saw bees, even a yellow jacket, but none heading toward me. I was as certain of the coming of the bee as the presence of the Voice itself.

From low on the grass on my right I saw a simple, battered, colorless bee coming toward me. It rose up high and sure enough landed on the big toe of my right foot. From its perch it squarely looked at me. I was astounded.

I was hyperventilating as I stared into the beady black eyes of the bee that stared right back at me. I braced for the sting.

"Where is your faith?" challenged the Voice.

"Please!" I cried aloud, abashed, believing a sting unnecessary to make a point. But that was not the point.

The butterfly remained peacefully still, continuing its stare through me. The longer I watched it, the closer I came to embracing the notion of faith, but my gaze on the bee stirred my phobic anxiety. Perspiration rolled off my neck. If faith was what the Voice wanted, faith I would muster. And faith I tried amidst my fear. In a desperate attempt to show courage that I could sustain a sting, I proclaimed, "I have faith! I have faith!" But I was confusing courage with faith. My words rang hollow. They were not yet spoken from a deeper place of understanding, that unchallenged place in the heart that does not need proof of anything; that place where scientists do not search nor do they dwell.

"Where...is...your...faith!?" spoke the Voice with the deepest compassion.

To find such faith while the bee sat on my toe necessitated recognizing the depths to which my fears ran—all my fears. Fear was the barrier to faith. This seemed to be the hardest lesson, but I was learning. *Faith conquers fear*. I knew the bee would not sting me now in the presence of such faith. And with this thinking I was instantly released from the turmoil. As both the bee and the butterfly remained poised on my toes, I also came to realize that *with faith there is a greater capacity to love*.

A spiritual door had opened. In my complete surrender, love poured through me like I had just received some Holy Blessing. This was as much a treasured moment as the love I had experienced from the Being of Light before that loving embrace collapsed into fear by what I could not understand. This seemed to be life replaying itself, but this time my eyes were open. I saw so clearly that it was neither the Figure in childhood nor the bee in any garden that had been the source of my torment. It had been me. Through life it had been me tormenting myself. In all the years from childhood to walking into this Garden I had learned nothing—until now—about finding or trusting the greatest Force within.

"I have faith! I have faith!" I repeated over and over. "My God I have faith!" I confirmed.

In review of this event, startling facts were realized. The Voice did not refer to this Garden as 'a' garden or 'the' garden or even Richard's garden. The Voice referred to this Garden as "His" Garden—the possessive pronominal adjective "His" meaning this Voice's Garden. Not knowing what name this Voice went by, or if this was God Himself, it didn't matter. If this was God—the acronym in Hebrew is YHVH—the hallowed name of God was never to be spoken anyway. Upon this Light of understanding I was instantly remade.

The bee and the butterfly remained unmoved on my toes. Staring at them, the dawning of faith in me was born like the creation of a universe. In the presence of such faith, there can be no doubt. In this moment, faith in a far higher Power than me, a far more Intelligent Power than me was born. I was in the wonder of it all. *What Intelligence is so grand that it can move nature like this? What Force has such immeasurable love that it can take a life so small as mine and hold it up to such Light? Whose Mind is capable of knowing my very thoughts, fears and life's experiences? And whose Mind has the ability to address my fears with such compassion and understanding?*

What a gift. It was almost unfathomable, but profoundly real. Its embrace around me was solid like the earth beneath my feet. In fact, it was exactly like Pastor Jack had expressed when he had bounced his cane. The Voice was more real than the very chair in which I sat. My fears put to rest, a courage rose in me unlike anything I'd ever experienced. With no hesitation my heart was open, receptive, vulnerable to this Great Source who spoke Truth and Wisdom.

The Voice had gone silent. Like my mother who had survived the incursion without a single sting, and only mud mistaken for blood, I too survived. I took in slow, deep breaths and released them. Upon each exhalation I felt released from a lifetime of resistance, ego-satisfying desires, fears and faithlessness. I stared back at the bee and the butterfly beautifully perched on my toes. Their peaceful loving eyes were still locked on me. Any other perception of them than exquisite beauty was a misperception. These small and loving creatures had become my biggest heroes.

"Thank you, thank you, thank you!" I whispered over and over to the bee, the butterfly and the Voice. I was so humbled, so honored for what had just transpired, and in reflection, grateful for the protection of my mother from so many decades earlier. The fact that she had escaped being stung was a true miracle in itself, and miracles I would now be welcoming. If this Spirit could move nature in the way it had just done, I knew it could have also done the same to protect my dear mom from a single sting.

The children across the street giggled amongst themselves, lost in their own world as the bee and the butterfly took flight together about a foot in the air between my feet. They circled each other in a celebratory dance and landed, this time the butterfly was on my right toe, the bee on my left. These mighty spirits looked at me just long enough, like a kiss, before they rose again to perform a spellbinding ballet around one another. They circled and chased each other high above me with lightness and gaiety. Then, they flew higher into the air zig zagging their way over a tall hedgerow disappearing from view.

In the wake of this experience, I understood the simplicity of trusting God. *The path to conquering fear is faith.*

CHAPTER TWENTY-SIX

My breathtaking experience in the Garden had been a complete transfiguration. I likened it to an almost bioelectrical firing of consciousness at some kind of soulful, cellular level. I knew that nothing would ever be the same again. How could it be? I got thinking about how those in the Ancient of Days must have felt when profound and mysterious events unfolded right before their eyes without understanding any of it. I was inspired.

I picked up Pastor Jack's New Testament, not seeking the indoctrination of religion but rather searching for content that might shed even greater light on my numinous experiences. I began on page one. By the time I finished reading the full Gospel of Matthew I realized it substantiated some of my own direct encounters.

It was late evening and I was awash in fatigue, exhausted from the emotional content in the reading. I called it a night. I turned off the lamp beside my bed, closed my eyes and in minutes I was asleep.

Sometime in the middle of the night I was stirred awake. Through squinting eyes I noticed a very bright light on in the room, but I distinctly recalled having turned off all the lights. I rolled over, opened my eyes brighter and was thunderstruck. Standing on the floor diagonally out about seven feet from the foot of my bed was a fiery column with real live flames licking the surfaces within the structure. It was fully translucent, seemingly glass-encased about seven feet tall and two and a half feet wide. Despite the flickering flames it generated absolutely no heat. I quickly sat up. The sheets and blankets fell from my shoulders. There was an inspiring wonder, curiosity and mystery about this column of fire. Whatever it was, it was enchanting. Fascinated, I stared in awe. I almost had to pinch myself to realize I was fully conscious and experiencing this.

My body glowed from the reflective orange light that cast the same radiance everywhere in the room. I expected to hear a voice—maybe even the Voice—but the room was absolutely silent. The top of the column and the sides were perfectly flat and cylindrical through which perhaps fifty orange living flames of fire danced within. They continuously licked the edges of the framed encasement never extending beyond the columnar clear glassy-appearing surfaces. It reminded me of a stoked furnace, yet unmistakably still devoid of heat. I looked on, mesmerized and fearless.

In about a minute, the sides of the column very slowly merged together. The further the two sides of the column collapsed unto itself, the darker the room grew. Then the other two sides collapsed inward, ultimately forming a beam of light standing seven feet tall with only dim light cast about the room.

Slowly, the single glowing orange beam started melding into itself from both top and bottom ends causing the room to grow progressively darker until it was reduced to only a pearl of light that floated in the air from the same relative position where it all began, about seven feet out from the foot of my bed. I couldn't take my eyes off the object. Upon a single blink of my eyes, the pearl of light disappeared and just as quickly the room fell dark.

Although completely mystified by this otherworldly event, one thing was so clear. I was fearless. Undaunted, clear-headed and not yet understanding the implications behind this column of fire, I laid back down and fell asleep.

CHAPTER TWENTY-SEVEN

When I next opened my eyes, with that sixth sense kind of knowing, I knew that a new mission about to unfold was going to bring answers. I abandoned the pleasure of a morning shower. Time was of the essence as I raced around the house getting myself together. I notified Doris that I'd be coming in on my own time to do some personal work for the day.

On the twenty-minute ride to the clinic I went over my many enigmatic events: appearance of the vessels, especially the fabulous crown jewel and its cloud extending over my sister's and parent's house; the cherubim choir with angels who may have saved my life on the freeway; the bee, butterfly and Voice in the Garden; and most recently, that fiery column. They were all seemingly meaningful pieces to a mystifying puzzle. I just needed the thread to tie it all together.

A rush of adrenaline shot through me. I was both exhausted from too little sleep, yet exhilarated by a new idea. In some unfathomable way might the Bible in its historical context hold a key that could unlock mysteries of my own events correlated to events from the Ancient of Days? I knew that research studies I'd conducted occasionally made no sense until unlocking that one missing statistical perspective that put everything else into logical order. This new possibility felt like it was operating on its own heartbeat.

I was on the hunt. I knew my metaphysical experiences had been orchestrated by an Intelligence far greater than me. I just needed to put it all together. Unshaven, disheveled and a bit weary, I plowed through the waiting room of the clinic.

"Good morning. Hi. Good morning," I said graciously to various patients in my froggy much-too-early morning voice. I flew past so quickly patients weren't quite sure it was me.

I opened the door to the interior clinic where Doris had just hung up the telephone. She looked up at me with a doubletake. "Richard!" she declared, catching herself before more surprise fell off her lips. "My! Look at you. Was it a head-on collision?"

I laughed at Doris's jibing. "Just on the run."

"Who's chasing you?"

I chuckled again. "Me, myself and I! Is Jim in yet?"

"No, but he should be here momentarily."

"Good. Keep me off the schedule for the whole day. I've got to get through this personal stuff. It really can't wait. Like we talked about, please let the trainees handle patients for me today."

I went to my computer station on the other side of the room where a pile of notes and patient charts awaited. I nudged them aside and sat staring into two side-by-side blank Apple computer screens thinking how I'll best approach my search. While I pulled on my beard, what was in front of my face suddenly jogged a memory. I gasped. It all came back to me in an instantaneous flash. When I came out of that lucid dream, floating in front of me were Adele's divining rod and the two blank computer screens side by side. I smiled. Had I at last understood the significance of the two blank screens? Indeed, it was on my lap to figure out what to do with them.

I was excited. "Doris, would you please get Computer Focus on the line. Ask Ted if he carries a program with word-finding capability on both the Old and New Testaments."

Without moving her body, Doris slowly rotated her head like a marionette, slightly cocked to the side. "You said…Old and New…the Bible?"

I timidly peered over the rim of my glasses. "Yes! The Bible. Is there a problem with that?" I queried, holding back a laugh.

"Land sakes! In all these years I didn't know you were religious!"

"Doris, I'm not! I have an idea and just need to look something up."

"Do you want the King James version, the Phillips Modern English, the Revised Standard—"

"Doris! Just ask Ted if he has any word-search software program on any combined Old and New Testaments."

"Okay," she replied, laughing and thumbing through her Rolodex, talking under her breath. "I can't believe we're having an inspiring conversation."

"How do you know so much about the Bible, anyway?" I queried.

"I've collected old Bibles for years. I have one that dates back five-hundred years. Each publisher can give their interpretation and one Bible can report the opposite of another. Now, for example, the Phillips Modern—"

"Doris!"

"I'm dialing. I'm dialing! I'm so excited for you."

I could feel the same excitement, but for an entirely different reason.

Doris called over to me. "Computer Focus has a software program for the King James Bible with word-search capability."

"Great! Have Ted send it over please."

In short order the software arrived. I lost no time performing searches. The wheels of the hunt were grinding. The software requested a response: *Word or Phrase Search?*

I typed the phrase *Column of Fire,* wondering if such a thing might possibly be in either Bible. The search came back: *Not Found. Suggestions? __Yes __No.* I clicked on *Yes.* Then the screen lit up with: *Pillar of Fire? __Yes __No.* I was bowled over. Could this possibly be the same pillar? I clicked *Yes.* The program processed pillar of fire and showed every citing where it appeared. Only six verses came up. I scanned down the screen. One verse stood out. Nehemiah 9:12 (Old Testament), *And in the night I leddest them by a pillar of fire to give them light in the way wherein they go—*

Massaging my beard, I repeated the passage to myself and recalled from Bible study classes when I was a young boy that the term 'fire' in the Old Testament had been translated from the original Hebrew which represented 'the presence of God.' Could the 'light' referred to in Nehemiah more accurately mean 'knowledge' or 'illumination' to find your way rather than brightness? I was still stuck on if this was the same pillar. Was its appearance meant to be a reminder to me of the very presence of God? Had the pillar in some way interacted with me? If so, I had absolutely no such recollection.

I focused on reconstructing an interpretation of that biblical sentence based on my direct experience: *And in the night I led them by the Presence of God to give them understanding in the way they search.* This made sense, but was I fooling myself?

I cued up *Angel*. The monitor showed one-hundred and ninety-two verses. I read several while it was all printing. Exodus 32:20 (Old Testament), *Behold, I send an Angel before thee, to keep thee in the way, and to bring thee into the place which I have prepared.*

I grabbed a dictionary and looked up *Angel*. It read, *Messenger of God.* I was convinced that the night of my near-disaster on the freeway was not my time to die. I was certain that the exceptional orchestral beauty of that holy choir had certainly saved my life, or at a minimum, a terrible crash.

I flashed back to the Palm Springs cloud that was no cloud at all. I typed in *cloud*. It showed fifty verses. From the printed sheets I read: Isaiah 60:8 (Old Testament), *Who are these that fly as a cloud....?* There it was. My own direct experience of the Palm Springs cloud right off biblical pages with the same question I myself had asked: *Who are these that fly as a cloud?*

I read Matthew 24:30 (New Testament), *Then the sign of the Son of Man will appear in heaven, and then all the tribes of the earth will mourn, and they will see the Son of Man coming on the clouds of heaven with power and great glory."*

There could not be a better description than *power and great glory* for what Lorene and I witnessed as the vessel glided across the night sky. I had to stop and take a breath. I sat back in my chair focusing on my breathing. I wasn't religious. I wasn't prone to take leaps forward from dogma and jump onto someone else's bandwagon. I needed a solid basis and rational thinking. Making links to my events would be easy, but would they be correct or would it be false equivalence? I held off on any judgments about this.

I read 1 Thessalonians 4:17 (New Testament), *Then we who are alive and remain will be caught up together with them in the clouds to meet the Lord in the air, and so we shall always be with the Lord.* I seemed to have fallen into a stupor. I found myself just staring at the screen. This verse was stunning to me because it was imbued with deeply religious interpretations, especially if I was to accept it as factual and relevant to present day. However, the fact that a cloud perhaps like my group had witnessed was described in Scripture, and there are apparently people residing in the clouds—*them in the clouds*—was enough confirmation for me to be clear that no one is going to be living in any clouds, but rather residing in some vessel within clouds. Both common sense and my direct experience indisputably confirmed this. An unanswerable question was whether what I had witnessed was in fact what our biblical ancestors had also witnessed. However, the most compelling albeit unanswerable question was if I had come alone to Palm Springs, would I have been invited aboard in love, friendship and brotherhood? I believed so.

I released a low frequency hum and continued speculating. Might it be possible that there are incalculable numbers of intergalactic craft all around the Earth waiting for the right moment, trigger or event to take certain people aboard—*caught up together with them in the clouds?* Perhaps the faithful? Are we in that period of history when 1 Thessalonians 4:17 is fulfilled? It could be consistent with "you will create a landing base." Although my logical mind considered this preposterous, I sat back again, took in a deep breath and remembered the maxim, *all things are possible.* This was beginning to feel like an archeologic excavation for ancient artifacts. I was inspired. What event could possibly cause us to be caught up together with them in the clouds? My thoughts stirred with half biblical verse and half intuitive reasoning. If Thessalonians was to be taken literally, then it's predicting a future event. If we are *to be with the Lord,* then we'd have to be taken aboard. Is this the time or is it yet in the future? If it's to happen, is it around a spiritual crisis or something more like a mass extinction event? Was I just shooting darts at a wall or could this be figured out?

My effort to connect dots could be false equivalency, but one thing was for sure. My group and I could not be isolated cases of witnesses. I intuited with an unexplainable knowing that what we had experienced was occurring all over the world in quiet, peaceful, spiritual transfiguration of our species. I knew this for one simple reason. While my many and varied experiences were indeed special, I was not special. Therefore, there really could be a case for the faithful being invited in one way or another to participate in a very subtle, quiet, almost underground spiritual revolution with Off-Planet Intelligence(s) right under everybody's noses.

My peripheral vision caught Jim racing around and heading toward the conference room, but I was hyper-focused. Nonetheless, Jim shouted over, "Hey Richard! Curt called and said that the rising audiometric curve you came up with was like finding the missing link. He's working on developing this further on Monday or Tuesday."

I smiled and waved to Jim vividly recalling that very special classroom during my lucid dream when the graphic audiometric image appeared on the chalkboard.

My fingers scrambled across the keyboard and typed *Voice*. The computer showed four-hundred and fifty-six verses. I was flummoxed. It had more frequently appeared than any other single term I had yet searched.

During the printing I randomly read a verse: Acts 9:7 (New Testament), *And the men who journeyed with him stood speechless, hearing a Voice, but seeing no one.*

I read another, Proverbs 8:4 (Old Testament), *Unto you, O men, I call, and my Voice is to the sons of man.*

And another, Jeremiah 7:23 (Old Testament), *Obey my Voice and I will be your God, and ye shall be my people, and walk ye in all the ways that I have commanded you, that it may be well unto you.*

I couldn't help wonder who but those who've experienced this Voice would ever believe its presence. I had an intuitive sense that what I had been experiencing, although brand new to me, appeared to be part of a very long religious world history. While the printer ground out pages, one phrase kept repeating in my mind: *Where is your faith?* I keyed up the computer and typed. It returned only one location where it appeared. Luke 8:25 (New Testament), *And he said unto them, Where is your faith? And they being afraid wondered, saying one to another, What manner of man is this, for he commandeth even the winds and water and they obey him?*

Stunned again—the dots seemed perfectly connected. This was right out of my own experience. Had the bee and the butterfly been commanded and manipulated by the same Force which the wind and water had been manipulated in the Ancient of Days? Had I not already been familiar with the Voice, I too would have asked, *What manner of man is this, for he commandeth even the bee and butterfly and they obey him?* Was this the same Voice? Was I being challenged in the same way as in the Days of Old? If so, this might suggest a Master Plan into Fellowship because I would hardly be the only one being challenged. I knew with an inner knowing that this was inclusive of masses of people across our planet finding themselves spiritually challenged with their own transformative events, maybe with the assistance and love of Off-Planet Intelligence(s). Might Hoova and other civilizations be doing this work behind the scenes?

Jim darted from a treatment room back to the conference room. I ejected myself from the desk and followed him. Trailing behind me were long linked computer pages. I found him at a table where he started laying out data sheets.

"Jim, check this out. I think I may have discovered something."

I laid down the first few pages of a connected string of sixty-five continuous sheets of freshly printed biblical verses. "Look here. The cloud some of us saw, I told you about, I think it's mentioned right here in the Bible."

"In what?"

"The Bible."

Jim laughed. "Richard, hold on, hold on. I've got data to tabulate."

"Wait. Wait. Look here." I excitedly flipped pages to my red notations in the margins. "Luke twenty-one, twenty-seven, and then shall they see the Son of Man coming in a cloud with power and great glory."

In a hushed voice Jim uttered, "This is nuts."

I smacked Jim across the shoulder. "Come on man. Look at this. I'm finding some correlations. This is based on my experiences, not dogma. I think I can tie a few of these things together. Numbers eleven twenty-five: And the Lord came down in a cloud and spake unto him."

Jim got up, closed the conference door and leaned against it. "No one spoke to anyone!"

I never shared a thing with Jim about the Voice—for the obvious reasons—except that I had received a telepathic invitation to Palm Springs. "Jim! I told you about the cloud our group saw. It was unlike anything we'd ever seen. And it wasn't a cloud. I think there's real spiritual implications here."

"I'll say! Overnight you've become a preacher's son!"

"I'm not talking religion. It's about history, humanity, maybe our future."

"Hold it, hold it. You're not a Bible scholar."

"No one needs to be a Bible scholar to understand basic English. I feel like I'm holding a piece to a puzzle that—"

"Look, if your reputation goes to hell, I go down with you by association. I brought you on board for your scientific talent, not existential cosmic bullshit! If any of this craziness escapes our clinic we'll be seen as looney tunes and we'll never publish! This is my livelihood! Yours too!"

"I get that. But this is my personal journey, Jim. No one needs to know."

"You're tabulating biblical data when you should be tabulating our data, work that puts food on your table too."

"I'm on my own time."

"You should be on our time!"

"This couldn't wait!"

"You're going to make a fool of yourself!"

I was a bit rattled, but I wasn't ready to give up even if he was going to remonstrate his way into a full-blown skirmish. The old Richard would have never considered these notions. The old Richard would have, just like Jim said, been afraid of making a fool of himself. In fact, the old Richard had already died without notice.

I continued. "Thousands of years ago who the hell understood stars in the sky during the day, clouds hiding aircraft, and a vessel lit up like New Year's Eve? Remember I told you about that one? The crown jewel vessel?" I watched Jim bury his face in his hands.

"It's all subject to personal interpretations, Richard."

"Yes, and it's highly symbolic, Jim. What does it mean? Hasn't it crossed your mind?"

"Of course it's crossed my mind—to not think about this or talk about it because it's beyond understanding. The risks are too great!"

"I'm clear about one thing. Hear me out! There's a world within each of us that is unexplored. Untapped. It's inextricably linked to the future. Our future! Everybody's future. There are forces at work far beyond our imagination and some of these vessels and the intelligences within them have an integral role in our lives. Our consciousness. Our history. And yes, our future."

"Now you're Bible thumping. These things could be a freakin' Air Force exercise and you're making it sound like the Second Coming! We have zero evidence or proof of anything. You don't even know what you all were witnesses to! Or did you throw objective science out the window?"

"This is phenomenological science. It's solid. I'm telling you there's far more here than meets the eye and if we want to find the truth, Jim, we have to get out of our own way. That means stepping outside the constraints of our beliefs, no matter what they are, if we're to look at the evidence. The truth. We both do that in science every day, but we don't apply it to our personal lives. Can't you feel that void?"

"I have no void! And I certainly don't believe in God if that's where you're taking this! This is nuts!"

"But I'm a witness to the—"

"None of you know what you saw! Wars have been fought over what people think they see!"

"Look, I'm not trying to prove anything here. I'm only—"

"Then why are you in my face with it?"

"Because I've discovered a, a—"

"Discovered?"

"Yes discovered! A spiritual force!"

"Oh great! Now that's a profound statement from a scientist! A spiritual force. Next, you'll be inviting me to a revival meeting. Come on, Richard! You can't be objective!" he argued. "You can't see past what you want it to be! This is ludicrous!"

"It isn't! My assessments are based on direct experiences which are—"

"Which are not objective! They're anecdotal experiences! Put this into a scientific framework!"

"It fits. Like I said, it's phenomenological!"
"No it isn't, it's one case study!"
"There were multiple witnesses to multiple events!"
"Did you tabulate the experiences of the others?"
"Of course not. I wasn't running an experiment!"
"Exactly!"

While I gathered my printouts, Jim grumbled to himself. I swept my hand down across my eyes and beard, took in a quick breath in this stalemate and backed off. I was burned out. Emotionally spent. I was compelled to share deeper understandings with Jim, but with his complete lack of firsthand experiences and with such resistance while only skimming the surface, I realized how little sense it would make. It was a pointless argument. Unwinnable. You'd have to be a witness and the last thing I wanted to do was lose a colleague and friend. Realizing the futility of the argument, I shut down, imploding on my own excitement. I recognized the wall Jim had built around himself—too high, too wide, too safe to consider anything outside the box. In fact, with all the walls surrounding him, as I saw it, he was now boxed in.

Following a big sigh, Jim pushed the long printouts aside looking for his data sheets underneath. We exchanged no further words on this matter. I hastily collected biblical printouts and wished I could tell him the far deeper story that had occurred in the Garden with a butterfly, a bee and a *Voice!* That would be nothing short of laughable to Jim. It was ironic that the one thing that had most transformed me wasn't even translatable into an intelligent conversation without sounding—like Jim said—ludicrous.

"I put the analysis of variance on your desk," he said. From the changed tone in his voice, I could hear my colleague hope that he hadn't been too hard on me. "Take a review of it and let me know your thoughts."

I was only half present. Jim's concept of life was based on stats and mathematics while my world was upside down, inside out guided by a deeper river of understanding. I felt like screaming, but in my frustration I realized there was no way to convey to Jim or for that matter any other naysayer the spiritual lessons one garners. They're probably nobody else's lessons but for those who experience them. It was no different than my experiences with the Figure at age nine when I tried to make my parents understand what had happened to me was real. I wanted Jim to consider the impossible and take a risk, to stop denying what wasn't in scientific terms observable, measurable and repeatable, and reach beyond the wall, but for whatever reason, it wasn't his time. I saw my old self in Jim as he rambled on. "Once you give me the correlations you calculated last week, I can input them and get with Curt on the next step if he has time—"

I placed my hand on his shoulder in a gesture of forgiveness and friendship.

My mind was simply swimming in a different universe. Once at my desk to pick up the balance of my work, I took note of the Old and New Testaments. I thought I had closed them both before I spoke with Jim. The Old Testament was opened to Ecclesiastes 3:1-8. *To every thing there is a season, and a time to every purpose under the heaven: A time to be born and a time to die; a time to plant and a time to pluck up that which is planted; a time to kill and a time to heal; a time to break down and a time to build up; a time to weep and a time to laugh; a time to mourn and a time to dance; a time to cast away stones and a time to gather stones together; a time to embrace and a time to refrain from embracing; a time to seek and a time to lose; a time to keep and a time to cast away, a time to rend and a time to sew; a time to keep silence and a time to speak; a time to love and a time to hate; a time for war and a time for peace.*

On my way out I stopped at Doris's desk. I was curious.

"By chance—" I smiled. "Did you happen to open the Old Testament on my desk to that wonderful verse?"

She looked confused and without her typical smile. "No."

I instantly believed her. "Someone left me a wonderful passage to read."

"Lovely. Wish I had time to do that!"

"Thanks, Doris, for always lending me support. I couldn't get through a day without you. You know that."

"I know that, Richard. Thank you for saying that. And don't take Jim's perspective to heart. He means well," she said sympathetically, certainly having overheard at least some of the kerfuffle. From the way she looked at me I suspected she had never quite seen me like this—totally resolute with a focused intensity on something other than clinical or scientific work. "Where are you off to?"

"Home, Doris. Home. I've got a lot of questions. A lot of questions need a lot of answers."

Once in the car I got thinking about how the world is so distracted that it may not even see the coming Light—bright as it will be.

Sex. Food. Fears. Regrets. Possessions. Television. Telephones. Money. Career. Work. Aspirations. Politics. Social engagements. Distractions are as endless as the human imagination.

152 The Voice

CHAPTER TWENTY-EIGHT

Dusk had fallen when I turned onto my street for the final stretch home. About two blocks south, a tremendous ball of light flashed from east to west low across my visual path and was plainly visible against the darkening sky. Once I turned into my driveway the enormous ball of light was hovering high above the west side of my house. It certainly had my attention.

I ran across the street to the Anderson's house and pounded on the door. Gene was quick to answer. Out of breath I looked at my neighbor. "Gene! You've got to see what's happening out here. It's crazy!"

"What's going on?"

"Look what's in the sky above my house!"

Pam and Johnny heard my excitement and came running to the door. All three then exited the house and stood with me gawking at the huge ball of light above and behind my house. The sun had set maybe twenty minutes earlier so the contrast against the sky was brilliant.

I had an idea. I turned to Gene. "Can Johnny help me out for a minute?"

"Sure!"

I instructed Johnny to alert everyone on his side of the block to get the neighbors out. He charged off with eyes glued to the sky. I ran down my side of the street and began knocking on doors. I wanted witnesses to see this for themselves and draw their own conclusions. I excitedly raced door to door and without realizing it, found myself pounding on doubting Thomas's door.

Kevin's father Larry opened the door, said nothing and just stood there. I knew he was still on the fence about what he'd seen with us, but I didn't want him to miss this opportunity. He saw my fervor and joined me.

A crowd was already gathering in the street between my house and the Anderson's. Maddie was there; Johnny was on his way back and there were more than a dozen other neighbors rushing over. There was a growing commotion on the street and lawns when we all gathered. A few strangers got out of a car and were stunned.

Larry and I arrived side by side with Kevin behind us. There were about twenty-five people gathered. When we reached the crowd Larry saw neighbors pointing to the huge ball of light. He was puzzled and confused, but he took in the sight. After a few minutes, without a word between us, there was a tacit exchange. It was just a nod of acknowledgment between us.

At this point Johnny screamed and pointed, "Look over there! Three more!" Sure enough, not very high over us coming from the east and heading west was a spherical vessel lit up like New Year's Eve. It was reminiscent of the Palm Springs vessel, but smaller.

Kevin shouted and pointed. "Look over there!"

Another vessel dressed in white light came from the south and arched in the air, swinging around high above us.

I saw a sixth one. "Look!"

This one was arching low over us and to the north. Sometimes a vessel would stop and its spherical shape was more detectable. Soon, everyone was pointing in one direction or another and hollering. At any one time we were able to see about eight to ten vessels. However, at no time did we hear any sound coming from them. In maybe ten minutes or less their flight pattern transitioned into a circular formation right above our street. The bright multi-colored illuminated vessels glistened. The widest diameter of circular motion was at most a mile; typically much less.

After half an hour, Pam was fed up with what she was seeing, believing none of it. "This is absurd! These can't be UFOs! Those are balloons or something with lights on them!"

"Balloons can't speed around like that!" Gene insisted.

"And balloons don't have lights on them, Mom!" Johnny added.

"Yeah, Mom!" Maddie said tenaciously.

"You guys are all nuts! I'm going back to the house to finish making dinner!"

I wanted to plead with her to give it a chance, but I could say nothing. This was an opportunity I suspected most people all over the world would have welcomed and Pam was casting it off as a hindrance to a hot dinner she was preparing. When she left, her father approached on his way to join the group.

"What's going on?" he asked.

"These guys are all out of their cotton-pickin' minds, Pop!"

"It's a celebration, Grandpa!" Maddie said with glee.

Logan, jumping up and down, reached toward the sky. "Look at all these UFOs!"

Mrs. Kretchmeyer joined the group. "Those things sure are perky!"

Maddie pointed to one of the vessels doing zigzag maneuvers seemingly less than a thousand feet above us. "Hey, Mrs. Kretchmeyer! They drive like you do!"

All the vessels emitted colorful light emanations and continued in a silent circular flight pattern. At one point about ten vessels appeared to be circling low over the neighborhood. Suddenly, a blood-curdling scream clearly audible to us was emitted from Pam inside her house. Our crowd grew instantly silent as all attention was on the Anderson's entryway. Pam body-slammed open the screen door almost crashing over the railing on a dead run for her life out of the house.

"Gene! Gene!" she screamed hysterically as she raced toward him, sobbing, reaching him, bolting into his arms. "Something grabbed me in the kitchen and pushed me out of the house! Oh Gene, I don't like this! I'm so scared!"

Pam's arms locked around her husband and didn't let go. Although Gene tried to soothe her, she was frightened as a child, clutching him, crying in panic, immobilized by her fear. Her vulnerability was palpable. I knew exactly what that felt like—terror initiated by what you do not understand; misinterpreting an existential moment based on raw human emotions. While I was fearless in the presence of these vessels, it saddened me that Pam's introduction to an extraterrestrial presence would require such frightful interaction. I held deep compassion for her, but it made no difference. She remained wide-eyed and quietly consumed with fear.

I tried to make eye contact to offer some kind of reassurance, hoping she might sense that I understood this kind of fear. But she was caught in her own nightmare. "Pam, I don't think they meant any harm by what they did. I think they just wanted you to be a witness."

Gene nodded appreciatively.

Over the ensuing hour the crowd continually thinned until I was standing alone on the curb peering into the sky, my vision fixed on the repetitious circling of the vessels. Finally, even I left to return to my house quite exhausted from the evening's events. I had a light bite to eat, washed up and went to bed.

Sometime late into the night I became conscious. I felt I wasn't in my own bed. There was a cooing of what seemed like hallowed voices. Was I dreaming? I seemed to be able to see through my closed eyes. I was resting in some kind of chamber safely within a structure that embraced me. In the presence of the cooing, I realized Beings of Light were standing around me aglow with golden light so bright they could not be clearly seen. They were well over six feet tall. I heard deeply expressive murmurs with the kindness, love and curiosity one might have for a child.

I was fearless. I sensed I was among family. I had an instinct unlike anything I'd ever felt before. Information came to me without spoken words. It was as if Light itself was knowledge. A realization came to me of this connection: *as above so below.* It felt like I was with my heavenly family. This was the group to which I belonged and every human was part of their respective heavenly family. Everyone is connected. Everyone. It only requires one recognizing the connection.

Those nearest my feet disappeared into the dimness leaving three others only a few feet away looking at me. Infusive light was everywhere. The Beings had flowing translucent bodies, but otherwise seemed very human. They wore golden light around them like sacred garments. It was like the golden glow I'd seen among those at the hair salon during my restored eyesight. It was a self-illumined presence. Through their hair and above their head, just like at the salon, rays of this light wove together like silky fabrics and the same glow emanated from their fingertips, brightness that disappeared into the thin, crisp air. Their every motion was slow. By contrast to the salon, their faces were so illuminated that their features were not discernible. Time seemed transmuted.

Operating on pure instinct I held an indescribable love and reverence for them that crossed all barriers of time, space and physicality. An intense radiance of light extended upward from their shoulders and into the air. There was something about their presence that seemed eternal through their love and this connection.

Suddenly, the cooing grew into a choir, seemingly emanating from within as well as external to me. I knew the eternal song. The brighter I smiled, the louder sang the choir. Was this the ensemble that had saved my life that night on the freeway?

One Being slowly approached me and in so doing, I observed a full dusty trail of light behind each motion. He wore a full beard of crystalline light that flowed down from his face and dissipated. I could not distinguish any details or features. I felt naked and vulnerable, yet, I was completely open, fearless and in awe. Between us a brightness flared out wherein I received the deepest essence of compassion and love. I was taken by its depth of penetration through me. This sentient Being spoke.

"Honor the Living Light within you and the Light glorifies in God. Then the Eternal Light becomes yours as it is ours. Listen and understand. War rages in the heavens beyond your perception in a battle for the Will of Man. As you surrender your Self for the Greater Glory, you shall see that we have always been with you doing the Will of God. Those from the outer world have created circumstances for you to use your very own Will against yourself through which the world remains enslaved. Willing against your Self is the foundation for the Grand Deception whose revelations must be revealed before our return."

I was so struck by this alarming message that I sat straight up in the structure only to find myself sitting straight up in my own bed at home. *What just happened?* Had this been a dream? Was it another lucid dream? Was the origin of this message from beyond the veil? Was this coming from an Angel, a Being of Light, an extraterrestrial, the Watchers? My mind was reeling once again.

I put these challenges aside, flicked on a light and scribed every word of the discourse indelibly etched in my memory. Once I put the pen down, I still did not know what to make of this. After I had awakened from my very first lucid dream, at least there had been a level of validation by the presence of a holographic vision that included Adele's divining rod and the computer screens. Here, I had nothing but a memory. Rather than write this off as meaningless, I dug my heels in and analyzed the full discourse.

Surely this group had already demonstrated to many of us that they're here or they wouldn't be reaching out through contact. They want us to see them or they certainly wouldn't be showing their vessels to so many. They want to be acknowledged among us or they wouldn't be communicating with us. I had an intuitive feeling that these are peaceful spiritual warriors who do not kill to conquer. They open hearts, eyes and minds to raise the vibration of the human Spirit.

We humans are exceedingly susceptible creatures to conditioning, indoctrination and false beliefs. At the time of my actual childhood encounter, terror around the unknown was already a programmed response from TV and movies about monsters and aliens. Pam's horror by what could have been well-meaning extraterrestrials was another example of a programmed response. Were these not evidence of the level of fear we humans are capable of that lead to willing against ourselves? While fear can serve as a protective mechanism, like not putting our toes to the edge of a three-thousand-foot cliff, it's a detriment if it leads to willing against ourselves. Fear is probably the greatest barrier to the raising of Spirit within that would otherwise take us to a Higher Vibration, to the Higher Threshold, to Ascension.

Willing against ourselves—self-deception—in the context of this discourse remained fixed in my mind. I asked myself, what is it we might be doing in our belief system that would prevent this Heavenly Family from making themselves known to the world? There could be many scenarios that address this question, but at the top of my list was the raw emotion of fear woven into our way of thinking.

Therefore, it seemed possible that one aspect of the Grand Deception may be woven through the fear of the very presence of those who love us, maybe even those coming to help us if in fact there is to be a landing base—but help that would not require worship of those here to lend assistance. My childhood encounter was a reflection of just how deep fear runs, deep enough to unwittingly repel the kindness, love and compassion of a higher form of life reaching out.

On a "Grand" scale, in metaphor, I imagined a great hand of compassion coming from the heavens and reaching down, but we are too frightened to grab hold, even warned against it. Thereby, perhaps what could result could be "Willing against your Self." In the end, this might also be willing against our true nature of Spirit within, so we must become the fearless.

The statement *"...revelations must be revealed before our return"* also tied in with the telepathic message about a landing base. Might this imply that they cannot make their presence fully known to us until enough humans across the planet have collectively awakened to the blunder in our thinking and correct such misunderstanding? While it might seem to be an impossibility that such awakening could ever happen quickly, I felt to my marrow that it could happen in the blink of an eye. I speculated that after our error in judgment represented by the Grand Deception is realized on an individual basis by enough planetary citizens, it could be enough to reach global critical mass for transformation. This in effect could be the long-awaited quantum shift. That is, simultaneous presence and awareness of Spirit within which leads to igniting Lights of Consciousness across our planet. I knew all too well that this could only be achieved by opening our hearts and minds, arriving at a renewed understanding of Off-Planet Intelligences and recognizing the true power of faith.

Honor the Living Light within you and the Light glorifies in God. Then the Eternal Light becomes yours as it is ours.

I understood that every human being is a Living Light. It is the Light of God. We are born with it and it can never be extinguished nor destroyed by oneself or by anyone else. Suicide does not extinguish it. It is a gift from the Eternal. How did I know this? I just did. It wasn't coming from a transmission. It was coming through understanding. Some dim the Light so low it is barely visible. Some Beings raise the Light so bright they're physically illuminated from within. Most of us do not even remember we're holding this Light. When one becomes aware of this Light that is ever present but hidden until conscious awareness ignites it, this seemed to be a direct pathway to God. This Being of Light was revealing not only that they have obviously already made this remarkable discovery and journey, but they're now assisting others in recognizing their own Light; turning on their Light. I saw that if we want to eliminate personal suffering, we must embrace our Eternal Light and sanctify the internal connection that is everyone's rightful heritage.

Listen and understand. War rages in the heavens beyond your perception in a battle for the Will of Man.

This idea was startling. Exactly who was battling whom? Was the armada of fourteen vessels I had witnessed part of this battle? Who did that fleet represent? How would we even know who is friend and who is foe? Was that going to be left up to intuition? How was it that I was even made privy to their presence? Would deeply spiritual warriors go into battle to destroy and kill their opposition? Isn't that counterintuitive to living life through the compassion of God with a fiduciary responsibility to the creation you love? If true, then this would seem to be a war among unawakened creatures potentially battling over any number of issues. One issue might even include breaking down barriers which in the past have limited human access to Higher Truths.

If it's beyond our perception I deduced the obvious. It is occurring in space and well off the planet. Another intuitive impression came. Designing advanced extraterrestrial craft capable of surmounting time and space that make it to Earth and then crash seemed to defy common sense. What would it be about Earth that would cause such vehicles to crash? Perhaps this discourse just made that clear. Was it more probable that a war beyond our perception has been the cause of downed 'UFOs' with a downed craft retrieval program long in place? Battling for the Will of Man suggested that certain forces have created circumstances for us to do what we believe is in our own best interest and perhaps the world's best interest, but in fact may be an atrocity against mankind, the planet, Spirit and God—like financial gain before common sense; war and killing in the interest of Darkness; fears that strangle spiritual growth. If all this is happening beyond our perception, it suggested that certain forces are manipulating our world in ways which we have little to no knowledge, let alone control over, unless just possibly the next statement offered elucidation and our way out of this manipulated drama.

As you surrender your Self for the Greater Glory, you shall see that we have always been with you doing the Will of God.

I intuited the more veiled messages. This Being of Light was suggesting that the choice to give up more and more irrelevant and temporary pleasures in life, from ego to possessions, and to give more and more of oneself to the Living Spirit within—*the Greater Glory*—this is the Light that gets turned on. This is the Light that glorifies in God. This is the eternal energy of the universe that awaits within each of us and can only be accessed by opening the hidden higher treasures of the heart and consciousness. I embraced the notion that these Beings who have always been with us have been here from time immemorial, educating and teaching us as far back as the start of creation based on the threads of this discourse which are self-evident.

I further intuited that we've arrived at a point in time when not only one extraterrestrial group is present, but apparently a plethora of species are deciding what to do with this human race. The intervention with Pam shoving her out of her house seemed to show intolerance and impatience for humans who are willful, indignant and denying of the extraterrestrial presence such that Off-Planet Intelligence seems to be left with no choice but an alarming determination to rattle awake the human species. I imagined Pam's reaction on a grander scale and saw how panic, fear and helplessness will prevail among those who fail to open their eyes, hearts and minds. Those open to Higher Evolutionary Intelligence will be the fearless, the faithful and the loving.

CHAPTER TWENTY-NINE

In the morning I awoke before sunrise clearheaded with a focused purpose. There was a gripping urge deep in the well. I not only didn't dismiss it, I welcomed such inner guidance. This subtle nudging forward reminded me of the brilliant Persian poet Rumi who said, "There's a voice that doesn't use words. Listen." I was listening. It was directing me to my favorite place in California just north of San Francisco. I had sojourned to Mount Tamalpais for many years spending Christmas to New Year's enjoying the beauty of that very special mountain. Although it wasn't Christmas Season yet, I grabbed a quick shower, packed a duffle bag, and filled a cooler with veggies, water and fruit.

An hour into my drive I took note of a car that had been behind me for some time. I considered it might be a government agent. I laughed at my complete disregard about it. They may be successful at phone monitoring, video recording or surveillance, but they could never tap my ever-churning Spirit. As for those who tapped my phone, I had long forgiven them. It was what it was.

Five hours into the drive I passed through San Francisco, across the Golden Gate Bridge and soon reached Mill Valley at the base of Mt. Tam. I started my ascent up the mountain, driving through big leaf maples already changing to colors of the rainbow. I was the only car on the mountain. Thick undergrowth was everywhere along the sides of the road. Giant Douglas firs and ancient towering redwoods rose up and canopied a wide variety of conifers. As I passed a couple riders huffing and puffing their way up steep sloping hillsides, I remembered how these very roads had contributed to the birth of the mountain biking craze of the 1960s. Halfway up was where the 1967 'Summer of Love' spawned the Marin County Magic Mountain Music Fest with the Byrds, Doors, Jefferson Airplane among many others. The 100,000 attendees turned out to be a prelude to Woodstock's hundreds of thousands to gather two years later.

Sharp twisting turns and unguarded cliffs along Panoramic Highway finally wound their way directly up to a wide-open clearing leading to the highest point for parking at the base. It was early afternoon when I arrived. Exceptionally few cars meant few hikers. I might be isolated at the 2500-foot peak. I threw on some sunscreen and tossed paraphernalia into my backpack—gloves, a cap, scarf, snacks and water bottles. I put on my old funky leather jacket and started the climb up the steep and rocky footpath beaten down through the years by previous hikers.

After a slow and steady trek up, I arrived at what felt like the top of the world. I located an outcropping off the main narrow dirt trail on the western side of a bluff and set myself down at the base of a multi-story boulder. Only one tower of the Golden Gate Bridge was visible from this vantage point. I burrowed down into my blanket next to a manzanita outgrowth and made myself comfortable. It was so peaceful I could almost hear Mother Nature calling, "What took you so long?" The environ embraced me.

It was a semi-cloudy day, but plenty of blue-sky peeks around gorgeous elongated clouds floating low over my head. The view was an aerial one well above the thickening fog starting to blanket San Francisco far below. I took in what was viewable through the panorama of the city and out across the breadth of the Pacific Ocean to its horizon. This was National Geographic perfection.

I delighted in the sights and sounds all around me. Two redtail hawks with fully expanded motionless wings rode the thermals hundreds of feet up and away. A lizard walked onto my blanket, paused, looked at me, tweaked its nervous head a few times left and right then decided to hang out for a minute right beside my leg. I smiled and whispered to it.

"Hey little guy. You're so beautiful. Thank you for sharing your space."

The tiny lizard started his jerky head movements again, then quickly scuttled across the blanket into some low scrub to carry on with more important business. Smiles filled me. I closed my eyes and listened. It was the purest sense of perfection and harmony. Rustling could be heard in the manzanita undergrowth. It was alive with creatures that made their home there. Two hummingbirds zipped by, seemed to wave, and left just as quickly. The chirping of chipmunks and squirrels hiding somewhere in the shrublands could be heard carried across the backdrop of breezes weaving through the wild brush and across my ears. Calls from two red-tailed hawks still riding thermals high above me signaled special messages to one another.

I relaxed my body from the shoulders on down. I read a little. I watched the world around me from stillness within. I sat doing nothing but listening to the music of the mountain. I so welcomed the change and the calm. I had quieted my emotional and physical body as peacefully as I'd ever done. In this state of heightened relaxation, I recalled the special message from Guruji Krishnamurti during those May talks: *Search for silence between the thoughts. There you will find Truth.* It wasn't that the unremitting wheel of thoughts can even be stopped, but rather, effort around it slows the grinding, and the mind quiets. Gradually my listening dissolved from the breezes, birds and land creatures to that inner sanctum. With closed eyes I focused on breathing in the cool fall air. Relaxation was enhanced. Muscles in my body started to disappear. Awareness of my surroundings faded. Self-awareness seemed to dissolve into nothingness. My inner roar of tinnitus and noise was gone as it bowed to silence.

I was floating between alpha waves (10 Hz) and theta waves (6 Hz)—a place where the mind can fully sustain, utilize and control relaxation to achieve nothing, or answer spiritual questions, or bring healing to a specific location in the body. It is a technique of which the Maharishi spoke. I was drowsy, drifting as though out to sea. I was sailing. I was not asleep, but I was not quite awake. Any deeper and I'd be into delta (3 Hz) and off to sleep. In this state it felt like I was healing my body. It is a very delicate dance between alpha and theta. I envisioned perfection in my painful joints. I sent thoughts of wholeness to those I loved. I asked for forgiveness among those I might have unknowingly hurt. Somewhere in the process of release I slipped into the bliss of just being. This was nirvana or samadhi and I was in its stillness.

Time and joy passed immeasurably on the mountain until I realized it was getting cold. The sun was at the horizon. As I came back into full awareness, I brought back sweet tranquility and inner peace. I felt healing to my body and emotions. Upon taking careful notice of San Francisco around five o'clock, I observed thick fog rapidly winding its way up the hillside, faster and faster on each successive burst of a breeze. The sun at the horizon was below the clouds like a painter's canvas casting out orange rays and iridescent glows. It was all quickly fading into the haze. I sat and watched. The wind picked up with greater vigor and the temperature seemed to be dropping by the minute. A sudden chill found its way inside me. I started gathering my belongings, wrapped a long scarf around my neck, put on gloves and stood facing the sea of clouds making its more rapid ascent. I zipped my jacket and threw the blanket around me. Staving off the cold, I was absorbed in nature's wonder.

Like the arrival of Spirit, fingers of the fog began to hug me. I had been hoping for this rare opportunity. With eyes closed and my face speckled in the mist, I opened my blanket like the wings of an angel and just for that moment I was sure I could fly. What a perfect way to bid farewell to the mountain. "Thank you, Mt. Tam," I whispered over and over and over. "Thank you, creatures. Thank you, God. I love you all."

On my descent off the summit, I leveraged careful footing down the rocky cliffside. Darkness was rapidly closing in. I thought back to my two most impactful sentient experiences: the Figure at age nine and the Voice at age thirty-nine. Had they been one and the same? Surely it expanded understanding of being in the world—being more present. Love from the Figure in childhood who embraced me without so much as a whisper was as much a watershed moment as the Voice decades later speaking Truth and Wisdom. Both profound in different ways.

As my thoughts drifted to Jo, I could see her important place in my future as a partner on a journey together. I came to welcome the love swimming so boundlessly inside me and knowing to always hold her close in my heart. To this end I offered interminable gratitude to the Voice that gifted so much understanding. I knew my life might never have woven its path as it did had the Voice not risen to guide my way. While I still wouldn't put a name to the Voice, it had been a welcomed Source of Illumination. There was no doubt that its evolution rose out of my desperate yearning to experience the Divine. In fact, it was the spark that ignited the search.

When I reached my car, I felt renewed. I started the engine, turned on the headlights and began the drive down the steep and treacherously narrow road. My car was the last vehicle descending the mountain. In less than a few hundred feet of twisting turns I began to feel that feeling again. My body started with a tingling of nerves, then a constant, persistent state of chills. It wasn't the weather. I sensed a surge of energy building like a volcano about to blow its crater in some kind of beautiful wild eruption with the release of Spirit. I knew exactly what was about to happen and I welcomed it.

The section of the road I was winding down was dangerously narrow with no illumination across the entire span of the mountain. Death defying cliffs with no guardrails kept my tires dangerously close to the edge. Finally, I located a very short outcropping on the right where I quickly pulled over, parked and turned off the engine. I flicked on the interior ceiling light, raced through the console hurling out miscellaneous junk until I found a pad, not sure I'd even make it in time before the inflow and outflow of Spirit. My energy felt like a dam holding back the ocean; a welling up inside that was taking over my body. The walls of this dam were in fact collapsing. My pen and pad in hand, the Voice spoke with the gentility of an Angel.

"All the sages in the universe do not compare in knowledge to what you behold within. Listen to no other voices, no other words but yours alone, for within you are held all the answers to all the secrets in all the universes. Listen, and let God flow through. He will whisper you secrets you can tell no one. He will give you Truths only you will recognize. He will give you love only you can embrace. This is your God Self. Your connection to Eternal Light. Your way. No one else's. Listen for His Voice for He whispers to you, but His whispers are like the thunder of a thousand storms. Heed His every word and you shall become His breath. The eyes through which you see the world shall grow blind to the illusions around you such that using God's eyes you see only Truth, even at a glance. Soon you will need no eyes to see, no ears to hear. In the silence of the moment, you shall become one with God. This is the Great Cosmic Secret, the Great Cosmic Gift, for He embraces each of us in this same personal way. His way. There is no other way."

Upon the last notated word, I was in the center of a powerful calm. My gratitude was boundless. I had received this discourse while in full conscious awareness—not passing through any lucid dream. Also, I was being spoken to in first person singular and third person plural—simultaneously. Therefore, I saw this information as available to all who lay their eyes upon it. I was so humbled. Now I needed to grasp the greater depth of this transmission.

In the dark of night with only the overhead light dimly shining down, I began reading it over and over. What had been somewhat elusive before, suddenly began to take form. I sat intuitively interpreting and continued to reread it word for word, line by line, slowly, carefully, mindfully, until at last I could coherently, confidently, knowledgeably read between the lines.

"All the sages in the universe do not compare in knowledge to what you behold within." He was speaking to all who hear with the Spiritual ear. I was proof that you can read countless books on spiritual growth to gain knowledge, but little of it will benefit you until these Truths waiting to be discovered are applied in life. What this Source was implying was that soul growth through our collective reincarnations have been for the purpose of gaining spiritual knowledge. The highest purpose of spiritual knowledge seems to surely be, in one form or another, progressively more interaction with the Divine. Intimacy with God. It's an internal process. No one needs to reach outside themselves or turn to sage wisdom of an Adele. All we must do is learn to listen internally.

"Listen to no other voices, no other words but yours alone, for within you are held all the answers to all the secrets in all the universes." I was a slow learner. I had been slow to recognize this precious Truth and its connection to Light within. New to this kind of listening, this was now welcomed confirmation. Everyone has the same connection. It's all attainable by everyone through one's own direct connection and internal processing. The loving gardener and caretaker of the vessel, this sacred connection to Illumination within, is something we all must eventually come to realize is us. We are the gardeners and caretakers.

It was God who sent us out to pasture, graze, learn, achieve and bring back to Him what we have discovered. Wars over religion; battles over faith; killing in the name of God are futile distractions which would seem to perpetuate the reincarnation cycle until we can end suffering. When we return to Spirit and experience suffering we have caused others, we may become witnesses to the need to end our cruelty to others. The inner Light of God is the Guide, and the Super Conscience is always showing our way to peace. He is the One doing the whispering through our conscience as an expression of His Wisdom. My complex mystical experiences had already demonstrated that whispering does not always have to be in the form of language if we simply open the flow.

"Listen, and let God flow through." The emphasis again was on *listening*. It was clear that we must listen with the heart. It is the channel through which God initially flows through before any such messages would ever need to reach the ears. I knew that listening required stilling the mind. The only way to quiet the mind is through committed meditation and prayer becoming an integral part of life. Quietening the mind effectually enables the inner Spirit to rise, direct, guide and sometimes even speak. This was confirmation that *listening* is the doorway to the flow. In fact, listening is the flow. It is a sacred river we navi-

gate. A journey to the Light. A path to the Divine.

"He will whisper you secrets you can tell no one." I knew from just my recent experiences with the Voice in the Garden that revealing such secrets—like to Jim Stanton at the clinic—opened the door to the outer world of misery because the connection to the Divine is a profoundly personal one. It is an internal process of listening, not an external process of hearing or explaining. My path was proof that it is not always wise to jump outside oneself when certain Truths are only meant for the one receiving them.

"He will give you Truths only you will recognize." This was made so clear to me. Every soul is as different as a fingerprint. Even if two beautiful souls look to be identical, they're different. They have different paths. Each must be true to their own destiny. Therefore, Higher Truths that apply to one life may have little relevance to another. For this reason, we are all on our unique transpersonal journey. While it is a privilege to share the signposts of our evolving Truths and deeper mysteries, they may be ones *only you will recognize.*

"He will give you love only you can embrace." This suggested that the love of God is profoundly personal. Once we receive it, recognize it for what it is and are deeply touched and moved by it, our instinct will be to pass it forward. I flashed back to my encounter with Pastor Jack McAlister and the love that exuded from him. It was unmistakable. I knew in my heart that he had been touched by the Divine. I was inspired by him, and like him, I was finding myself passing love forward through more compassion and kindness. I was coming to understand that this family of Off-Planet Intelligence is here to stir the world. Stimulate us. Nudge us. Push and prod us. Remind all who need it. Some of these Intelligences will even correct our misguided paths, just for the love of God.

My thoughts turned to religion. It seemed to me that religions have become as complicated as the Tower of Babel. Vast numbers of us no longer understand one another despite our committed faith in the same religion and even under the same God. Judaism identifies God as Yahveh (YHVH). Christians in the past have used the name Jehovah to represent God, and more recently use YHVH when referring to God. Muslims believe in Allah, but Allah in Aramaic means God. Mormon fundamentalists call Jehovah their God, but in Hebrew, Jehovah means Lord and Lord is God.

Thus, it was apparent that Abrahamic religions, which comprise about half the world's population, all represent the One, the same and only God. It was becoming clear what Adele had said—religions separate us. I wondered what a world we'd have if all those who represent religious order held to a collective theocratic oath of bringing humankind together under the single Light of God. I flashed back to the earlier transmission through my lucid dream: *Imagine a world where the only religion is Truth from within doing work of the same God for all mankind.* Why hasn't our world ever come to embrace this Truth? Why haven't we, the citizens of this planet, come together despite which religion one posits if all who believe pray to the identical God, proven to be so by the very same holy name we hold sacred?

Sitting back and reflecting on the entirety of the discourse, I observed that the possessive pronouns 'He' and 'His' rather than 'their' or 'them' were repeatedly and consistently used. By logical inference and understanding its application to everyone and with no mention of a single religion, the implication was crystal clear as if I was mining it through my DNA. This was reaffirmation. One God for all of humanity; the same God personalizing appropriate messages to every single searching soul regardless of the name of the religion. Therefore, by logical deduction, to find our way Home, we cannot confuse the One as two (or more).

I dropped the pad of paper onto my lap as if dropping to my knees. My eyes were closed as I reveled in what felt like hallowed interpretations. I was so grateful for receiving this understanding. In a private prayer to all that is Divine, I expressed my appreciation for direction in my life, curved as it sometimes had been with unpredictable twists and turns, like the mountainous terrain upon which I sat. I took in a few deep breaths, picked the pad back up and continued reading the transmission.

"This is your God Self." Yes! We are the receivers, and in some cases the transceivers. This is the purest state of being. In human *being* there is no higher state of consciousness than *being*. Living in the state of Godliness is living in the I AM Presence. Living in one's conscience is the training ground for the God Self. It is the God Self in everyone that hopes to be recognized like a seed awaiting germination. We are the vessel that waits to be opened. Faith is its water. Religion merely identifies it, packages it, puts a name on it. When one is in harmony with this Divine Presence, perhaps this is the highest vibration attainable for a human being. It is the connection between God and Self. Perhaps it is even the purpose behind human birth that in itself originates from the Divine, but is so often lost after birth into the maze of illusions and delusions. Attaining the God Self is an internal process which cannot be accessed through the outer world. While influences from reading, rhetoric, religion or even lessons in faith can come from the outer world, the connection to the Divine can only happen within.

I had an immediate understanding that access to God is not a complex process. That would be illogical, perhaps even against natural universal law and make such essential access difficult for everyone. Accepting that God is accessible directly to all, one-on-one, with instantaneous compassion, then any intermediaries standing between the faithful and God would be unnecessary. I saw that the presence of thousands of religions and sects across our planet make the path to the Divine confusing—noise that masks Truth from oneself. Therefore, we may not hear the very Voice that whispers if it's masked by the noise of dogma, and especially if we're told we don't need to listen because someone else will do the listening for us.

Among all the thoughts the mind holds, it seemed none could be lordlier than one's conscience—the innermost thoughts, feelings and central voice that differentiates right from wrong. I was coming to see that when we come up against a moral judgment, it could be the very Conscience of God that whispers, *This way please I beg you.* Thereby, developing this Conscience—a higher connection—as if it is a muscle in the body appeared to me to be golden steps to the Sacred. Every thought, every decision, every word that leaves the lips through language must pass through the conscience as a spiritual process before it is ever spoken. I sensed that knowing this strengthens the inner voice—the God Self—to speak clearer and louder within. It is not unlike tuning in a distant radio station. Sometimes it can be audible. We must not forget that the conscience itself is a whisper giving options for direction, conduct, behavior and decisions, all operating under the domain of our Divine connection.

"Your connection to Eternal Light." Eternal Light is the symbol of Divine Presence. This tells us that Divine Light shines down through every soul. Once passing off our planet we become spiritual entities of Light returning to the Source while still maintaining our individual soulful identities. I have concluded that this must be true because our individual soulful identity is how we grow and learn through cycles of reincarnation. When each of us continues to cultivate our God Self, it strengthens our connection to the Godhead.

"Your way. No one else's." Understanding that every soul is different, then every Way—the individual Path you take in life—is different than anyone else's. Your life is your way. Something that had been hazy on my mind slid into sharp focus from the original message telepathically received: "…You will create *a landing base.*" I knew I hadn't been equipped to create any physical space for vessels to land. That was impractical. This seemed to be a metaphor. The message did not say 'the' landing base. It said 'a' landing base suggesting one landing base I would create. This could also have implied that countless other people all around the world are also creating 'a' landing base. In that case, we'd be talking about a mass landing of Off-Planet Intelligence. While I saw that as certain in our relative near future, I saw that *'a landing base'* could be interpreted as a double entendre. Might it have been allegorical, meaning *to receive*, like landing a deal or landing rights to something? If my interpretation of this metaphor was correct, then *landing* also meant embrace, as in embracing spiritual change, which in my case proved to be the *landing of faith;* that is, a landing base for the presence of the Divine. I suspected that millions of people across the planet are experiencing much the same thing. This then would suggest that a global spiritual Awakening is underway. This shift will move us from separation among people back to faith's original purpose of connecting mankind to the Eternal Light of the Divine.

"Listen for His Voice for He whispers to you, but His whispers are like the thunder of a thousand storms." An astonishing realization came to me. The Voice in the Garden was in every respect the thunder of a thousand storms when the bee and butterfly had interacted with me. The fact that the Voice once again used the possessive pronominal adjective "My" Garden when referring to my garden further confirmed this Source. Furthermore, it was the third time the term *listen* was stated in this discourse and it was not used colloquially. The reference was not to hearing nor even to the hearing organs themselves. That reference throughout the discourse was to the internal process of listening. Listening offers the opportunity to understand. It's listening for the inner wisdom held in the sacred chamber of the Temple within. *Temple* is derived from the Latin word *tempula* meaning how we process time. On the other side of the veil there is no time, so inner listening is the pathway to the infinite: the Divine. The awaited whispers come from the other side of this veil through the doorway of the conscience where free will decides whether to accept the communication and apply the wisdom. One thought can change the world.

"Heed His every word and you shall become His breath." The conscience within; the echoes in the hallowed chamber of the mind that whisper right from wrong; and obeying the Inner Truths as if your life depends on it are some of what comprise His every word. By living the Truth of God's wisdom from His spiritual guidance within, one becomes Truth. In so doing, one breathes the breath of God. This sanctified breath is Pure Light reflected like a mirror through our actions in the outer world. No one needs to know from where it comes. It only needs to be present and shine through thoughts and conduct. Breathing the breath of God will bring new vision.

"The eyes through which you see the world shall grow blind to the illusions around you such that using God's eyes you see only Truth, even at a glance." The outer world is an illusion. You often cannot trust what you see or hear in the outside world or the best intentions of others. No matter the source, everyone has their own agenda, misdirection, biases, false beliefs which can corrupt the Truth of what is. You can only trust what comes through the connection within which are the eyes that see Truth. Our eyes are God's eyes. Therein, as short-term renters housed in our volatile and diverse human shapes, we are using His eyes for our soul growth—a journey through the eyes of Spirit.

"Soon you will need no eyes to see, no ears to hear." This is the meditative state of consciousness that can shatter illusions because one is able to see without the senses when the mind is still and the heart is open. It is the magical state of being as close to nirvana as one can be while fully conscious where

thoughts are as noiseless as a snowfall. It parallels the sanctity of deep prayer.

I flicked off the light and collapsed my body back into the seat. I popped open the sunroof to welcome nighttime sounds of nature. I opened all the windows and could hear crickets chirp in combined rhythmic songs as breezes wove their way through shrubs, trees and everything around me. I stared up through the sunroof to the stars hiding beyond the impenetrable fog, sprinkled through the darkness of the heavens. The moon may have been coming over the horizon any minute. The cityscape may have even been viewable from this mountainside, but I didn't need eyes to see or ears to hear. I was in stillness.

"In the silence of the moment you shall become one with God." Is it the journey outward to the holy sites all around the world that await us, or is it journeying to the Temple within whose doors are always open and whose Light is always on? Between the temporal lobes on each side of the brain is where thought resides and where the connection can be made to the Divine state where God flourishes. Though the walls of any temple can collapse or a physical body will die, I now understood that Spirit within this Temple is everlasting. I knew I must maintain the God Self by keeping the mind still, peaceful and quiet so that when He speaks without words, I will hear the wisdom.

Detaching from the illusions in the outer world while maintaining the God Self creates the opportunity to receive all appropriate information at all appropriate times as life unfolds. This Truth applies to every human being. We cannot forget that silence in meditation and stillness of mind in prayer is the Pathway. The longer this Flame is kept bright, the stronger grows the connection. In essence, the physical body is the mere framework for the true House of Worship built to manifest oneness with the Divine. Our journey is our fingerprint that becomes our unique stepping stone back to the Eternal Light of God.

"This is the Great Cosmic Secret, the Great Cosmic Gift, for He embraces each of us in this same personal way." The Great Cosmic Secret, among many Secrets handed down in this instance, refers to becoming one with God by listening through stillness within. Secrets are whispered and whispering mandates quieting thoughts enough to enable the process. The "Gift" through listening is guidance from the Divine directly to the conscious mind. To the Self. Recognizing His embrace may even be the very nature of Ascension.

Countless numbers of people feel cut off, broken and abandoned by God. Somehow though, I understood that God abandons no one. Thus, as Sentient Beings made of the stuff of star dust, I've come to realize we too are Beings of Light who shine brightest when we find He who is ever present within. Such a moment is the deepest sense of *knowing* what you cannot prove. Faith. It is the comforting heat from the flames of fire that keep us warm on a cold night. However, if we do not approach near the ever-present Flame, it is not culpability of the fire that we are left out in the cold. The Hand from above is always reaching down within. We must invite, retain and grow our connection to the Divine no matter our condition of health, wealth, despair or tragedy. It is no different than the father of a family with innumerable children who embraces every child equally, each in their own personal way, with exactly the same impassioned and selfless love. However, we children must open our arms to receive the embrace of the Father. It is then that the seed of the God Self puts forth roots. If we accept that the DNA of God is in our physical structure when we subscribe to being made in His image, and we have not yet experienced the miracle of the Divine, then it is we who must make the invitation to Him to rise up within our heart and soul so we can know His love and wisdom.

*"**His way**."* This is gender neutral. It simply means the Divine way—the way of Light. Our journey does not work until it is literally Divine. We must show love. Compassion. Kindness. And all attributes that comprise Godly treatment of all living things. Keeping our Eternal Light bright will allow our Heavenly Family to see us shining. They will in turn nurture and protect us. I see this as the only way Home. The Divine way.

"There is no other way."

172 The Voice

Afterword

Earth, just a speck in the cosmos, is out among countless trillions of solar systems. It is separated by endless billions of galaxies seemingly lost in the far reaches of space. We are traveling through time and space at the rate of tens of thousands of miles an hour into an ever-expanding universe. This makes Earth our mothership. It's our home with gnawing questions that persist. *How irreparably have we harmed her as we continue to ride this great ship,* and *how much damage is coming from a natural course of our solar system's evolution?*

While invisible in the depths of the heavens, we are relevant enough to have Higher Evolutionary Beings working behind the scenes. They love us and this planet. If the message I received, "you will create a landing base" has a physical correlate, then we are on a countdown to a landing. Ongoing, bold, worldwide sightings are an indicator that this could be unfolding right before our eyes. We need to keep in mind that some species have influenced humanity in irresponsible ways while it appears that others are fighting for our survival. Now we must awaken from our slumber.

In the 1990s, Courageous Canadian Minister of Defence Paul Hellyer was very vocal (see: You Tube). He told us there are virtually dozens of different species in our airspace, the majority with our "best interest" in mind. However, he also said a few other species hold much less compassion. This is a reminder to use discernment if you participate in this arena, and most importantly, be sure your Spiritual House remains in order. This will be key to stabilizing Truth within.

Andrija Puharich's narrative in my story accounts for our early meetings. I often reflect on this bright, complex, enigmatic and fascinating man of mystery. In his travels from North Carolina to California in the latter 1980s and when he wasn't up north in Carmel, we occasionally got together before Jo and I moved to Sedona. We developed a mutual respect for each other on what seemed like the same track to Truth. By the time we had built a trusting relationship and although he may have once been an Intelligence-employed scientist, I felt he was no longer so engaged. In fact, I came to sense that he had become a tragic victim of his search for Truth. Controversy seemed to follow him with attempts even after his 1995 passing to slander his reputation and discredit his honest efforts.

His connection with the Nine through Dr. D. G. Vinod eventually returned him to the Nine a few years later when he met Phyllis V. Schlemmer who then also channeled the Nine for him. I could not help wonder if Dr. Puharich's Nine could be one and the same as the nine gods of the Great Ennead in Egyptian mythology. They were the gods worshipped at Heliopolis.

This might further illuminate Hoova's sentiments that we need to stop worshipping and fearing advanced species who come with extraordinary technologies to help mankind in our challenging times. We also need to stop the fear. It is self-annihilation and sustenance for that which is not Light. Chaos and disorder are the comfort of Darkness. Love, faith and compassion are destroyers to its presence. All we need to do is brighten Christ Consciousness within and prepare for the inevitable and pending Earth changes and coming Ascension.

In a compelling book by Schlemmer (see bibliography), one can recognize that she was an impressive and adept channel for Dr. Puharich. To understand the truth in Schlemmer's work, one might best read without preconceived ideas. The lead extraterrestrial named Tom, channeled through Schlemmer, told Puharich's group that a species will be coming to raise the vibration of our planet which is just another way of describing Ascension. The Hoova species among many may well be part of what we have been witnessing in skies around the world.

In an intriguing book by Stuart Holroyd (see bibliography) who was also included in Puharich's group of multiple witnesses and who audio-recorded various sessions, Tom reportedly said that those who've passed to the other side are apparently stuck in limbo unable to rise off the spiritual skin of Earth because of the density of our planet. Hence, the need to raise our vibration is once again a pressing point. Holroyd goes on to say in one session that Tom told Phyllis to share that Earth is the most beautiful of all the planets and that we have a moral obligation to preserve it.

Worthy of mention is Paramahansa Yogananda's masterful treatise on the Second Coming of Jesus (see bibliography). He postulated that the very Christhood Jesus discovered is available to all of us who seek it: *seek and ye shall find.* Yogananda saw that Jesus was the flawless example of discovering the Christ within—the Light of God—available to all souls. Might this have been the message Jesus taught among the Essenes which revealed lasting spiritual self-empowerment? Yogananda beautifully presents an understanding of this process of Christhood—resurrection of the Christ within you. While his postulations might at first blush seem to go against traditional Christianity, I did not find that. In fact, I found what he posits to be rather consistent with Hoova's transmissions through Schlemmer when Tom spoke representing the Nine. It happens to also be consistent with my direct experiences, spiritual transmissions and understanding.

As much of the world recognizes, Master Teacher Jesus clearly came as our example. In an earlier book written by Yogananda *(Autobiography of a Yogi),* he shares direct experiences he had with his personal master teachers who passed on; yet returned to him in physical form, witnessed by others. Such 'miracles' which are merely the universe acting in ways we do not comprehend, have been recorded in a variety of publications, especially in India through the Mahabharata, Bhagavad-Gita and other sacred texts. After the multitude of my experiences, especially the floating crown of a king and Dr. Puharich confirming Hoova can materialize a body as needed, the reality that Jesus could in fact return should not be taken lightly.

With respect to my personal interchanges with this Voice, it was not a traditional process of channeling. No part of my consciousness ever appeared to shut down. I never found myself to be in a trance. I did not relinquish any part of myself as would be expected with channeling which enables an independent source to internally speak in order to pass forward information through the mind of the one channeling. At no time did I ever intentionally (consciously) solicit these interchanges. These transmissions always came as a surprise. For me, it was simply listening with all my faculties intact. I was quiet. The Voice spoke. It was like answering the telephone. As such, I found it compelling that elements of what were revealed to me through the Voice seemed to be consistent with what was revealed to Dr. Puharich through the Nine including a physical landing. Many others have also received very similar information that pertains to a literal physical landing.

As I write these words, Lights of Consciousness are connecting across this planet. Connection-to-connection accelerates the process of our awakening. Each of us must do the work and hold the connections—the Divine within and the hands of those we love. We all are linked. Human to human. Human to Spirit. Spirit to human. Back and forth again and again, over and over we go until we rise up and out of this cocoon. While holding these connections watch what transpires through your illumination of love. Pay attention to your dreams and daily consciousness as you begin to see through the eyes of Spirit. You can expect both large and small miracles to unfold. They will prevail. It might be the simplicity of a butterfly landing on your shoulder at the most propitious and synchronistic moment. You may suddenly know something you had no way of knowing, therein confirming the presence of a Higher Order operating in your life. It could be a sudden flash of intuition that propels you to solve a mystery or save a life.

My highest hope is that this book will launch deeply personal conversations. Though you may want to share my story, consider this. If what I've revealed has triggered memories, do something with them. The truth of your own lifechanging spiritual experiences have value. Call together family, friends and neighbors. Your conscience won't lie to you when you consider with whom to share such pearls. Pass forward your deeply held treasures. If you've heard the Voice, now is the time to tell your story. You are not crazy! You may be pleasantly surprised how the most private spiritual secrets shared among cherished friends and loved ones will begin to open spiritual doors for everyone.

They will nudge memories in others which will inspire even more to share their moments, all of this accelerating the connections toward the Awakening.

This book began with Dr. Kochkin's thoughts, so it's apropos to conclude with his recent conversation with me. "We are all a single pixel in this big picture of a captive reality composed of eight billion pixels of various colors. Every time a pixel wakes up, shares, loves, forgives, evolves, grows up, integrates, worships, shines, I believe it has an impact on the entire big picture since we are all interrelated; perhaps we are even a single Being seemingly fragmented into billions of pieces. This is what I call the Great Cosmic Gestalt. That is, the dissolution of all illusions of "I" and "Not I" which will eventually liberate all souls from this oppressive dualistic concept of being; and thus, cause us to reclaim our Higher Identity in alignment with our Beloved Creator, so eloquently discussed by our favorite mystics, sages, theosophists and philosophers."

Epilogue

In the past 50 years, sightings and extraterrestrial contact have taken a significant shift. It has been on the incline with millions of people worldwide having irrefutable photos or videographic documentation. In the meantime, varying degrees of intervention and communication are ongoing. Some encounters have changed viewpoints; some have transformed lives. Countless other moments have left people speechless, without words to even express how they've been touched; and therefore, frozen in their state of memory—unable to tell their story. We are now entering a global transition into a New World. It is time to talk.

Margaret, a loving friend of mine and Jo's, stood graveside, heartsick over the loss of her mother. Weeping alone in the cemetery, she heard a male Voice come to her, gentle and soft, speaking within her. "It'll be okay." These little words of comfort so deeply touched her that her entire perception of God was transformed. Another friend, Gary, was traveling along local Highway 179 in Sedona approaching a blind curve when he too heard a male Voice come to him, in this case with frightening alarm. The Voice hollered, "Pull over! Pull over!" He was so shaken that he swerved off the road and slammed on his brakes. Immediately, a tandem timber lorry which had already lost its flatbed load on the blind curve, was hurling long freshly cut lodgepole pines across the entire road in his direction. Gary watched. Not a single log hit his truck. Brother Sergei Kochkin was touched by the Divine when he heard, "Grab as many hands as possible and bring them back to Me." We must continue to share. The more we share, the less fear we manifest, the faster we learn.

Perhaps by now you've been wondering why this story sat untold in my computer for forty years. It was not the right political climate and the story needed to simmer. Like a sculptor new to the craft when a master teacher plops down a mound of clay on an artboard, decades helped this story take shape. It had to make sense to me first. I returned to it frequently until I could finally extract enough sagacious insights from the unexplainable, even the supernatural. It was slow absorption of remarkable moments to a level I could talk and write about them without the risk of sounding incoherent, unbelievable, or adding unnecessary distortions and mysteries to an already confusing world.

Like life itself, people in my story moved on. Jo and I moved to Sedona in 1989 where people for years have reported profound life-changing mystical experiences. We married there in 1990 and were later blessed with the love of a wonderful daughter. I practiced 17 more years and founded a book publishing company in the hearing industry to continue educating those who suffer from auditory-related maladies. Jo provided psychotherapy to our community, then moved into facilitation with Northern Arizona Restorative Justice for first-time juvenile offenders. She's also on the board of the Sedona Int'l Film Festival.

Dion retired from audiology in 2020, married sweet Angela and continues to bike and hone his skills with a cue stick. Christopher moved to Northern California for a deeper dive into self-discovery. Unfortunately, David fell ill and passed away. Our dear Lorene was tragically stricken with a ruptured brain aneurysm and she too died after the turn of the millennium. Sid continued to battle PTSD from the Vietnam War and spent more time in and out of VA psychiatric care.

Rick Hurst still has the same humble heart and humor. He continues to make appearances around the country at Dukes of Hazzard events and has completed his first book of prose and true stories, *Totally Random Reflections*. It includes his own remarkable extraterrestrial events which began one year after our Palm Springs encounter. The footprint of Pastor Jack in my life has remained steadfast and permanent. Meeting him was a close encounter of its own kind.

The kids in the neighborhood all went their own way growing up and now approaching their fifties with children (and grandkids?) of their own. A few years ago, I drove to Los Angeles looking to see if any of the families still resided in my old neighborhood. Only Johnny's family was still there where he and his sister Maddie came back home to roost for a while. I got to chat with Pam and Johnny about the multiple UFO events they experienced with me on the street. Although all of us saw Pam pushed out of her house by the extraterrestrials that night, she said she had no memory of it. It's well known that significant trauma can block memories. In her living room that afternoon after I recounted the moment of her terror, Johnny almost fell off the sofa. Recapping it gave him the validation he had been so long craving. Right after the encounter he had tried to convince her it happened. Now three decades later he finally had the backing he had been seeking. "I told you, Mom! I told you!" Gene, Pam and the family apparently never spoke of the event again. Yes, indeed it happened, just like the Being of Light who had come to me at the same age when my parents too didn't believe it. These are evocative moments that instantaneously transform life. One is never the same again.

At the age of seventy-seven after I closed the cover on this final draft, inspired by Spirit, I looked up the meaning of my middle name. I'd never done that before. If I had I'm sure I'd have been mystified. However, once I looked it up at this ripe age, it hit me with the kind of twist that often comes out of one of those unexpected gifts hiding in plain sight. The Hebrew translation of Elliott is *The Lord is my God*. It was there all the time like **I AM**. I just didn't see it.

Acknowledgments

There were so many friends who contributed to commentary along development of my inconceivable number of drafts. Their critiques and feedback shaped how the story got told. I feel fortunate to have such loving family and friends, many who themselves were witnesses and who supported my efforts.

In 1987, when my fiancé **Jo Stone, PhD** began witnessing mindboggling events with me, it was she who adamantly insisted I write this story. Flabbergasted by unidentified aerial phenomena as well as extraterrestrial manipulated events, she petitioned her PhD committee to change her dissertation topic to 'alien abduction' (see bibliography). I'm so grateful to Jo for her many hours of feedback on my earliest drafts right up to the final, and so many decades of love and understanding throughout the challenges I faced talking about my most deeply personal experiences. If not for her love and encouragement, I can't imagine that I ever would have stepped from the shadows into this highly controversial circus. Jo has been one of the most important and inspiring women in my life. Her career choice, character and personal life reflect her truly noble spirit and perpetually open heart.

Anoeschka von Meck, PhD became a South African bestselling novelist in 2005 with her book *Vasilineje* which in 2017 won South Africa's Best Picture. I'm a very lucky uncle to have Anoeschka in my life with her deeply spiritual presence and as a partner in Truth-Seeking whose path intertwined with mine. As such a skillful writer and bestselling author, she was kind enough to help tighten the final draft. Her input was invaluable.

Dion Svihovec, PhD was Section Chief of Audiology at the Sepulveda Veterans Administration Hospital who invited me to assume a clinical position with him in 1978 and ultimately a research post. This was only four years after he and I were audiology trainees at the Los Angeles VA Outpatient Clinic. His long and close friendship was the open door that allowed me to share my very early drafts for feedback which I so appreciated. His brotherly love on our shared paths of the esoteric has meant the world to me. I'm not sure how my professional (let alone my personal life!) would have unfolded if not for this unique man so full of heart, wisdom and friendship.

Sergei Kochkin, PhD has been more than a mere colleague in audiology and brilliant contributor in my publishing company. The spark into brotherhood ignited immediately when we both discovered we were on the same journey; into the same searches—even the same music. I will always cherish our countless hours of discussion on purpose, direction, the Divine and existential matters that have enriched my life. Few words can adequately express my appreciation for this wise soul.

William Schohl was a copywriter and my roommate in Los Angeles in the early 1970s with whom I have maintained a life-long friendship. I so appreciate his copywriting feedback on my near-final draft. His honest commentary is what actually led me to expand and go deeper into my interpretation of the spiritual transmission I received while I sat in my car below the summit of Mt. Tam reading and rereading the download.

Paytone Delmars has been a loving friend for over three decades along with her husband Cailen ever since Jo and I moved to Sedona. As an avid reader, she had interest in the final draft to offer suggestions. Her feedback certainly helped to nudge and further open my heart. Thank you so much.

My sisters Joy and Joan became part of the early story for the obvious reasons of all of us living together as siblings in Syracuse. Joy and others in her home living only two blocks from our parent's house in Palm Springs were also eyewitnesses during the event. I thank my dear sisters for their love and encouragement throughout, and a special thank you to Joy for her strength to stand behind the truth of her own experience as a witness.

Erin Sax, my goddaughter, film director, singer and songwriter. Thank you for your never-ending faith in my work, and your contagious laughter through the many decades of this project coming to fruition. Such a kind heart!

V. J. Ransone has worn many hats—a broadcast news journalist in Washington, DC; a visionary; educator; and for over forty years an interdimensional communications investigator. As an ongoing adept channel, she received a telepathic extraterrestrial message in 1978 that she relayed to NASA's Space Shuttle team. It literally saved the lives of astronauts. We happened to meet quite serendipitously just six weeks before this book went to press. It turned out that she had been Dr. Andrija Puharich's research assistant in the mid-1970s. Thus, she was well acquainted with dozens of the program's 'star children' and implications of extraterrestrial contact for humanity. Thank you, dear Cosmic Traveler, for all you've done and for making a difference in this book.

Gisele M. Bonefant arrived on a parallel wave with V. J. Ransone. Thank you for your swan dive into the final draft with deep and thoughtful editing and doing so without hesitation. Your patience and kindness made a difference.

Alexander Volkov created the original cover design for this book. He was so kind and gracious. He came to the U.S. from Russia in 1960 and has achieved his unique thumbprint of success. He said that he learned from the masters. "They have all taught me something. How to see. How to hear. How to understand things. And most importantly how to understand myself. I cannot separate any one of their voices from the voice which I hear inside of me which has become my own voice."

Excerpts from Signed Sworn Witness Affidavits

Christopher Balazich {has been a close friend for decades, one who also has been on the challenging journey of life exploring the Higher Evolutionary Presence.}

I met Richard Carmen and our many other friends at Richard's parent's home in Palm Springs, California on the evening of Friday, October 18, 1985. I had come there at Richard's invitation as a witness. I had become distracted so that just after 2 a.m. when I realized something was happening outdoors and exited the house, whatever had occurred was over, so I missed it. I know that Richard and one of the female guests there witnessed whatever had been scheduled to occur at 2 a.m. They told me about it in quite some detail. The next evening, Saturday, October 19, 1985, around sunset I slept over at Richard's sister's home (Joy) where her step-daughter Anoeschka was also residing for the weekend. Both houses were only a few blocks apart. While at Joy's house, I took notice of a strange and huge spherical cloud almost directly over the house—I am guessing it was a couple thousand feet—a huge oblong shining cloud. I witnessed several small disk-shaped white shining craft darting in and out of the cloud.

Joy Carmen-Ullock, MBA {is my sister. She has been part of the corporate world since 1976. Through her successful real estate career as an Associate Broker for more than 25 years with Coldwell Banker Realty in Sedona, she has earned a number of achievement awards.}

My brother Richard Carmen told me that he had received a telepathic message that he should be at our parent's home....there would be an extraterrestrial event. On Sunday, October 20, 1985 around twilight I was witness to an extraordinary oblong cloud about a half mile wide that appeared over my home and extended over to our parent's home. It appeared to be around a quarter mile high. One-hundred percent of the perimeter of the cloud rolled off what appeared to look like dry ice vapor that quickly dissipated. Despite a breeze, the cloud remained unmoved through the night and into the late hours of the morning. I witnessed typical UFO vessels drop from the cloud, hover, sometimes three or four together, then shoot silently across the sky and disappear. I also witnessed the same or other craft come from the darkness, silently hover beneath the cloud, then rise straight up into the cloud and disappear.

Rick Hurst {well known for his role as "Deputy Cletus Hogg" on The Dukes of Hazzard, has appeared in literally hundreds of commercials, TV shows and feature films.}

I first met Richard Carmen in 1985. Sometime well before the date of October 19, 1985, Richard told me that he had been invited via a telepathic message to be at his parent's home because he was told he'd be a witness to an extraterrestrial event at 2 a.m. the following morning. I unfortunately was still in the living room and by the time I got to the back patio, literally minutes later, that event was over. Richard and his companion ... stated they did see an extraordinary craft lit up like New Year's Eve that followed yet another craft lit with only a single steady red light.

"Johnny" {is a pseudonym used to protect this 9-year-old's true identity. He was kind enough to provide a long affidavit. He's turning fifty now, so maybe this book will be the shoutout that inspires him to go public with our shared experiences.}

<u>First Event</u>: *One day it might have been me who asked Richard how we could get to see UFOs like him. He explained that it was very easy to do that if we just ate healthy, were positive and loved everyone. So seeing that he always ate salads, we went back to my house to make a salad. It was the first time I ever ate a salad. Then me, my sister ... and my friends ... went out on our front lawn and sat very quietly hoping that having eaten lettuce would help us see UFOs. It sounds crazy to say that now, but we were kids and knew no differently. We were shocked that in a matter of a few minutes, we in fact did see UFOs crisscrossing and weaving in and out of each other. We went and got Richard. He joined us on my front lawn and we were all witnesses to the same event. Silver UFOs or lights in the sky were dancing and darting around.*

<u>Second Event</u>: *Another time Richard came over ... asking if I would go knock on neighbors' doors on my side of street and have them come out and ... he did the same on his side of the street. I did just that and in a matter of a few minutes there were more than 20 of us standing out in front watching many UFOs flying around, darting, appearing, disappearing, like they were putting on a show for us ... I vividly recall that my mom had been cooking dinner that night and for whatever reason decided to go back into the house to finish cooking, not believing any of what she saw. The next thing I remember is she blew out of the front door, almost toppled over the railing as she came out screaming "something's grabbing me and forcing me outside!!" ... The strange thing is that no one in our family ever talked about any of this again.*

<u>Third Event</u>: *One day I happened to look out our window and saw a single UFO flying over Richard's house above the pine trees hovering silently maybe almost touching the top of the trees. He wasn't home, but I remember when he got home I ran over to tell him about it.*

Jo Stone, PhD {see acknowledgments}
When I met Richard he confided in me about the many extraterrestrial contacts and telepathic messages he had experienced in the preceding years. Intrigued, I wondered if I might be able to witness something myself, so he took me to an outcropping on Topanga Canyon ... and within minutes we saw what appeared to be a spinning, multi-color star in the dark sky moving in erratic ways that I just knew was beyond our earthly technology. There were other extraordinary events during this time witnessed with Richard that were mystifying and unexplainable unless one explained them by means of extraterrestrial intervention.

Dion Svihovec, PhD {see acknowledgments}
Richard soon shifted to heading up research [at the VA] *during which time he and I collaborated on pioneering research in tinnitus and metabolic disease. We have maintained a close friendship ever since. I was invited quite some time in advance by Richard Carmen to stay at his parent's home because he had stated he had received a telepathic message to come there to witness an extraterrestrial event at 2 a.m. the following morning. I unfortunately had fallen asleep in the living room and by the time I got to the back patio literally minutes later, that event was over. However, I am witness to a strange low frequency hum coming from above that immediately followed that event and persisted for about 20 minutes around the backyard that we couldn't figure out from where it was coming.*

Anoeschka von Meck, PhD {see acknowledgments}
On Sunday, October 20, 1985 just after sunset I was witness to an extraordinary oblong cloud about a half mile wide that appeared over Richard's parent's home. I witnessed typical UFO vessels drop from the cloud, hover, sometimes three or four together, then shoot silently across the sky and disappear. I also witnessed the same or other craft come from the darkness, silently hover beneath the cloud, then rise straight up into the cloud and disappear.

184 The Voice

Readings

Carey, Ken. *Vision.* Kansas City: Uni-Sun, 1985.
Carey, Ken [Raphael]. *The Starseed Transmissions: An Extraterrestrial Report.* Kansas City: Uni-Sun, 1982.
Hesse, Hermann. *Siddhartha.* Germany: S. Fischer Verlag, 1922.
Holroyd, Stuart. *Briefing for the Landing on Planet Earth.* Flagler Beach: Old King Road's Press, CreateSpace Independent Publishing Platform, 1979.
King, Godfre Ray. *The Magic Presence.* Chicago: St. Germain Press, 1935.
King, Godfre Ray. *Unveiled Mysteries.* Chicago: St. Germain Press, 1939.
Puharich, Andrija. *Uri: A Journal of the Mystery of Uri Geller.* NY: Anchor Press, 1974.
Schlemmer, Phyliss V. and Jenkins, Palden. *The Only Planet of Choice: Essential Briefings from Deep Space,* (second ed.). Palmyra: Salamander Books, LTD, 1993.
Stone-Carmen, Jo. A descriptive study of people reporting abduction by unified flying objects. In Pritchard A, Pritchard DE, Mack JE, Kasey P, & Yapp, C, (eds), *Alien Discussions—Proceedings of the Abduction Study Conference, Held at M.I.T.,* Cambridge: North Cambridge Press, 1994.
Waters, Ed & Frances. *The Gulf Breeze Sightings—The Most Astounding Multiple Sightings of UFOs in U.S. History,* NY: Morrow & Co, 1990.
Watts, Alan. *This is It (and Other Essays on Zen and Spiritual Experience).* NY: Vintage Books - Random House, 1958.
Yogananda, Paramahansa. *Autobiography of a Yogi.* Los Angeles: Self-Realization Fellowship, 1946.
Yogananda, Paramahansa. *The Second Coming of Christ: The Resurrection of the Christ within You.* Vols 1 & 2, Los Angeles: Self-Realization Fellowship, 2004.

Appendix
The Lessons

1. All things are possible.
2. We are not alone.
3. You cannot reap the benefits of a spiritual path you fear.
4. Not all Truths can be shared.
5. Each of us has a guardian angel, a guide from the other side, who protects and guides us. It can even be our master teacher. Our challenge is to listen.
6. Love and compassion must fill every moment.
7. It's so important not to condemn another person for what they believe or say or do or think. Do not judge people. We do not know why people do what they do or say what they say. Just forgive them and love them.
8. Life is a process that battles suffering with a fine line between the laughter and the pain. The line's an illusion. It's all but a single process woven into the fabric of living. It's what we do with suffering that matters.
9. Spirit materializes change in the world by movement of space. This is done through you and by your choice. Remember—space comes from Light, and Light is always guided by the love of God. Spirit can work within coincidence which is our way of reminding you we are with you. This element is Divinely inspired to better serve mankind.
10. To master light, you must master thought. When you learn the timing and relationship between thought and action, you will see through the window of Divinity to all the Sacred Truths. That's how Divine action occurs. Through thought. Through you. Living this wisdom will unveil lines of synchronicity that shall unfold patterns to you, such that you may even foretell that which is to come.
11. Imagine a world with no hatred or war. Imagine a world without need. Imagine a world not based on beliefs, but attuned to truth, hope, love, charity, faith and healing. Imagine a world where the only religion is Truth from within doing work of the same God for all Mankind. Imagine a world where dreams are real. This is the world that is here. These miracles have always been available.
12. Miracles occur. We must learn to accept them, embrace them, not challenge them. We must learn to give gratitude for each and every one of them.
13. The path to conquering fear is faith and with faith there is a greater capacity to love.
14. Honor the Living Light within you and the Light glorifies in God. Then the Eternal Light becomes yours as it is ours.

15. Listen and understand. War rages in the heavens beyond your perception in a battle for the Will of Man. As you surrender your Self for the Greater Glory, you shall see that we have always been with you doing the Will of God. Those from the outer world have created circumstances for you to use your very own Will against yourself through which the world remains enslaved. Willing against your Self is the foundation for the Grand Deception whose revelations must be revealed before our return.

16. Search for silence between the thoughts. There you will find Truth.

17. All the sages in the universe do not compare in knowledge to what you behold within. Listen to no other voices, no other words but yours alone, for within you are held all the answers to all the secrets in all the universes. Listen, and let God flow through. He will whisper you secrets you can tell no one. He will give you Truths only you will recognize. He will give you love only you can embrace. This is your God Self. Your connection to Eternal Light. Your way. No one else's. Listen for His Voice for He whispers to you, but His whispers are like the thunder of a thousand storms. Heed His every word and you shall become His breath. The eyes through which you see the world shall grow blind to the illusions around you such that using God's eyes you see only Truth, even at a glance. Soon you will need no eyes to see, no ears to hear. In the silence of the moment you shall become one with God. This is the Great Cosmic Secret, the Great Cosmic Gift, for He embraces each of us in this same personal way. His way. There is no other way.

18. There is one God for all of humanity; the same God personalizing appropriate messages to every single searching soul regardless of the name of the religion. Therefore, by logical deduction, to find our way Home, we cannot confuse the One as two (or more).